Tennessee
TITANS

Celebrating the First Ten Years

This book is available in quantity at special discounts for your group or organization. For further information, contact:
Triumph Books
542 South Dearborn Street
Suite 750
Chicago, Illinois 60605
(312) 939-3330
Fax (312) 663-3557

Printed in U.S.A.
ISBN: 978-1-60078-200-8
Design, Page Production, Editing: Red Line Editorial
Photo credits: Getty Images unless otherwise noted

Contents

CHAPTER ONE: **MOVING TO TENNESSEE** 7

CHAPTER TWO: **DECADE OF STARS** by Bob McClellan 13
Eddie George 13
Steve McNair 19
Frank Wycheck 25
Keith Bulluck 29
Bruce Matthews 33
Jevon Kearse 41
Derrick Mason 45
Craig Hentrich 47
Brad Hopkins 50
Samari Rolle 52

CHAPTER THREE: **SUPER SEASON** by Jim Wyatt 57
Yeah, It Was Preseason, But... 57
A Great Start 59
Titanic Showdown 60
Freaked Out 60
Reason to Celebrate 61
Music City Miracle 63
The Man Behind the Miracle 71
Racing by Indy 71
Dance Party 73
No Hot-lanta 74
Super Bowl XXXIV 74
Awards 84

CHAPTER FOUR: **GREATEST GAMES** by Jim Wyatt 87

Titans over Steelers in 2000 87
Titans over Jags in *Monday Night Football* debut 88
Titans Win at Washington on *Monday Night Football* 89
Del Greco Kicks Five Field Goals 91
Titans Grind Out Blizzard Win 92
Christmas Night, 2000 93
Last-Minute Field Goal Provides Win over Oakland 95
Titans Win 2002 Season Opener over Philly 96
Goal-line Stand Lifts Titans over Bengals 97
McNair Painfully Guides Overtime Win at Giants 98
Wild Win over Pittsburgh in 2002 Playoffs 100
McNair Has Record-Setting Day in Win over Houston 102
Goal-line Stand Helps Titans Hold Off Jags 103
Titans Rally to Beat Falcons 104
McNair Pass Caps Comeback Win at Houston 105
Titans Win Playoff Game at Baltimore in 2003 107
Big Day at Green Bay on *Monday Night Football* 109
Titans Rally to Beat Giants 110
Bironas' 60-yard Field Goal Beats Colts 112
Young Runs for OT Score in Houston Homecoming 114
Defense Scores Three TDs in Wild Win over Jags 116
Titans Rally to Win in Buffalo 119
Season-opening Win over Jags in 2007 120
Titans Shine in Prime Time at New Orleans 120
Bironas Makes Eight Field Goals 123

CHAPTER FIVE: **GENERATION NEXT** by Bob McClellan 127

Vince Young 128
Kyle Vanden Bosch 132
Albert Haynesworth 133

CHAPTER SIX: **JEFF FISHER** by Bob McClellan 137

MOVING TO TENNESSEE

As revered as Bud Adams is for bringing his NFL franchise to Middle Tennessee, he was reviled in Texas for years for having moved it.

Adams was a founding member of the NFL rival American Football League that began in 1960. His franchise was the Houston Oilers, and the team started with a bang, winning the first two AFL titles and reaching the championship game again in its third season.

In 1965, the Oilers were scheduled to play in the brand new Harris County Domed Stadium, the first such structure of its kind. But Adams rejected the terms of the lease at the last minute, and the Oilers played at Rice Stadium for the next three seasons.

It was just the first hint of trouble in a rocky relationship between the city of Houston, its pro football team, and the team's owner. In the absence of the football team, the stadium was named after its baseball tenant. The Oilers finally worked out their problems with the lease and

LP Field before a game against the Atlanta Falcons on October 7, 2007. (Photo by Wesley Hitt/Getty Images)

The Astrodome was home to the Houston Oilers prior to their move to Tennessee. (Photo by Getty Images)

began play in the Astrodome in 1968, but the team hit the skids. Was it an Astrodome jinx? In the eight seasons prior to going under the roof, the Oilers compiled a record of 57–53–2. In their first seven seasons inside the dome, they were a miserable 29–64–4, including consecutive 1–13 seasons beginning in 1972.

Coach Bum Phillips led a resurgence in the mid-1970s. He took over in 1975 and immediately led the Oilers to a 10–4 mark. His reign hit its crescendo from 1978-80, not coincidentally the first three seasons after the team drafted running back Earl Campbell with the No. 1 overall pick. With the powerful former University of Texas star eating up chunks of yardage, Houston reached consecutive AFC Championship games, only to fall to the powerful Pittsburgh Steelers in both 1978 and '79. The Steelers, of course, went on to win the Super Bowl both times.

The Oilers went 11–5 in 1980, capping three consecutive seasons of double-digit wins. But they lost in a wild-card playoff game at Oakland, and despite a record of 59–38 under Phillips, Adams fired him. It was another move by Adams that didn't go over well with the Oilers fan base. Not only had the homespun Phillips made the team a winner, but his wit and wisdom had also made him a favorite throughout the league.

He seemingly took the firing in stride, remarking that there were two kinds of coaches, "Them that's fired and them that's gonna be fired."

Adams' disdain for the Astrodome grew while his team suffered through some lean years after Phillips' departure. In 1987, the owner threatened to move the team to Jacksonville, Florida, unless improvements were made to the dome. At the time it seated only about 50,000 for football, making it the NFL's smallest stadium. City officials didn't want to cave to Adams, but they didn't want to lose the NFL either. The city responded with $67 million in improvements that included new Astroturf, additional seating that pushed the capacity past 60,000, and 65 luxury boxes. The funding came from increases in property and hotel taxes, as well as bonds to be paid over 30 years. Adams, in turn, promised to stay in Houston for the entire length of his new 10-year lease in the refurbished dome, beginning in 1988.

He didn't keep his word. By 1994 he already had launched a campaign for a new stadium with a retractable roof and club seats. Mayor Bob Lanier collided with Adams. The politician had hoped to keep the Oilers around, but he eventually took a hard-line stance against any public funding of a new stadium for the football team, a stance he made public in July 1995. Adams fired back. He sent a letter to Lanier's home, telling the mayor he would move the team if the city didn't come around to his way of thinking by Aug. 1.

Lanier went public with Adams' ultimatum. His decision made Adams furious and essentially sealed the fate of the Oilers in Houston. Adams didn't take kindly to a public rebuke any more than Houstonians had enjoyed his flirtations with other potential markets. Adams began secret negotiations with then-Nashville Mayor Phil Bredesen. At the end of the 1995 season, Adams announced he would be taking his team to the Music City for the 1998 season. City officials had agreed to pony up $144 million toward a new stadium and guaranteed $70 million in ticket sales.

"I've said it all along, Nashville did what Houston didn't," Adams said. "The only way I could be a part of a deal, and compete with the new stadiums going up around the league, was to come to Nashville. They've been very good to me and I want to do what we can to be successful here for a long time."

There was the not-so-small matter of the Oilers' remaining two years on their Astrodome lease, however. Lanier threatened to make them fulfill it. "We have bought and paid for them," Lanier told the NFL owners at their meetings after the 1995 season. "It's like buying 10 loads of cement and you only get seven delivered. We just want the other three."

After oft-contentious negotiations, the Oilers and the city of Houston reached a settlement that would allow the team out of the lease. Adams paid $5.25 million, and he agreed to drop a lawsuit over a 1995 canceled preseason game in which the team had been seeking $2.5 million to $3 million in damages. Meanwhile, Oilers officials floated a plan to play at the Liberty Bowl in Memphis during the 1996 and 1997 seasons while the stadium in Nashville was under construction. It was hardly the ideal situation, but it would allow the franchise to play on Tennessee soil.

> **The only way I could be a part of a deal, and compete with the new stadiums going up around the league, was to come to Nashville.**

Legal issues held up the move, and the Oilers played the 1996 season in Houston as lame ducks. It was a disaster, an embarrassment to the franchise and the league. The Astrodome became the world's largest mausoleum. Crowds dwindled to less than 20,000. The team preferred being on the road, going 6–2 away from Houston and 2–6 inside the dome.

After the season, the city agreed to let Adams out of his lease a year early. The new stadium in Nashville now wasn't going to be ready until the 1999 season, so the plan was to play the 1997 and 1998 seasons in Memphis. The team was headquartered in Nashville, and everyone made the 200-plus mile commute on game days.

Everyone, that is, except for fans who lived in Nashville. Adams overestimated the appeal his team would have that far away from its intended home. He underestimated the rivalry between Memphis and Nashville. Memphis had been trying for years to get an NFL team of its own, and it became apparent that pro football fans there weren't all that interested in a lame-duck team either.

People stayed away in droves. The Oilers' regular-season debut in Tennessee, a 24–21 overtime victory against the Oakland Raiders, drew just 30,171 to the Liberty Bowl (capacity: 62,380). Raiders coach Joe Bugel during the week had called it a "neutral field," and while the Oilers toed the company line the Oakland head man essentially hit the nail on the head. Five home "crowds" were less than 28,000. The Oilers drew less than 18,000 twice. If it wasn't quite the embarrassment the final season in the Astrodome had been, it resembled it all too closely.

Adams had every intention of playing in Memphis during the 1998 season as well, even as difficult as the 1997 season had been on everyone involved. But the final regular-season game, against the Pittsburgh Steelers, forced him to rethink the plan. The largest crowd of the season—a respectable 50,677—had come out. The problem was the overwhelming majority had come to root for the visitors. It was more or less Memphis' salute to Nashville.

Adams decided it would be better to play the 1998 season at Vanderbilt Stadium on the campus of Vanderbilt University. The capacity was only 41,000, well below NFL standards, but the Oilers had only had one crowd larger than that in Memphis. And at least they would be playing in Nashville. It wasn't ideal, but if someone had said, "Give me Liberty (Bowl) or give me death," most of the team would have opted for the latter.

Finally at home in the Music City, the team got off to an 8–6 start and was in the thick of the playoff hunt before dropping its final two games. Just before the season began, Adams announced that the team's name would be changed to coincide with the opening of the new stadium and to befit its new location. But he also said the renamed team would retain the Oilers' history and records, essentially taking one last swipe at Houston by keeping it from reclaiming the name and records for an expansion team, as had been the case with the Cleveland Browns some years earlier.

At a news conference on Nov. 14, 1998, Adams announced that the Oilers would begin the 1999 season as the Tennessee Titans. Their official colors were to be navy, titan blue, white, and red. "We wanted a new nickname to reflect strength, leadership and other heroic qualities," the owner said.

The team's new logo was unveiled five weeks later, with a nod to the three stars on the state flag of Tennessee that stand for the different land forms in the Volunteer State— mountains in the east, highlands in the middle, and lowlands in the west. The logo featured the three stars in red around a white "T" that formed the head of a comet with light blue and red comet trails.

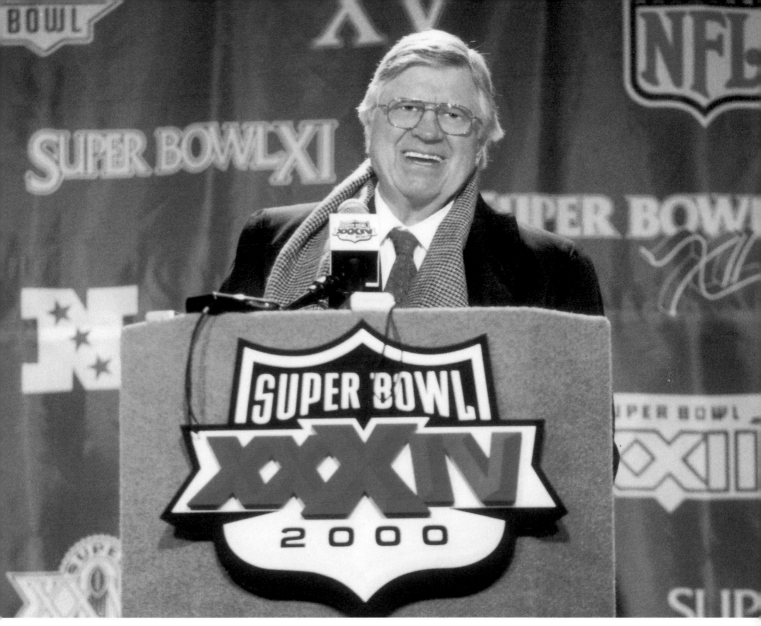

Titans owner Bud Adams. (Photo courtesy Tennessee Titans)

"I feel we have developed a logo that fans throughout the state of Tennessee and around the country will embrace for years to come," Adams said.

The name also paid homage to Nashville's nickname as "The Athens of the South." Now it remained only for the team to open its new stadium and to play like Titans.

DECADE OF STARS

by Bob McClellan

EDDIE GEORGE

Eddie George was the embodiment of what Jeff Fisher wanted his offense to be. He was a hulking 6'3" and 235 pounds, with the body of a Greek god and the work ethic of a blacksmith. He ran downhill nearly every time he touched the ball. If there was no hole through which to run, he would hit it anyway and take defenders with him.

It was a near-perfect fit. Fisher was schooled in playing close to the vest. Run the ball, control the clock, control the game. The coach needed a workhorse, and with the 14th overall pick in the 1996 draft, he found Secretariat in the Heisman Trophy winner out of Ohio State and saddled up.

"As we were building the team, he was perfect because we were developing a young quarterback. When you develop a young quarterback, you need to run the football and rely on someone to run the football and steel that mentality," Fisher said. "We emphasized the run game and the toughness and it allowed us to create an identity."

George started every game of his eight-year career with the franchise—128 regular-season games and nine postseason games. He had an average of 21.4 carries per game for his 137 career games

Hard-running Eddie George fit coach Jeff Fisher's system perfectly. (Photo courtesy Tennessee Titans)

with the Titans. He carried the ball more than 300 times each of his eight seasons, and he delivered more than 1,000 yards in seven of them. He topped the 10,000-yard rushing mark in his final game as a Titan, becoming at the time just the 17th player in NFL history to reach that mark. "I'm just so blessed and honored to be within that group," George said.

Among the Titans he was in a class by himself. He was as reliable as a sunrise. He was a crutch for quarterback Steve McNair until "Air" was ready to breathe on his own. He was a security blanket for Fisher, because about the worst thing that could happen when George got the ball was 2 or 3 yards for the Titans.

"Eddie always wanted to know what he could do to be better or to help us win more games," Fisher said. "So many impressive plays and games, but the thing that comes to mind for me is our opener in our inaugural year in Memphis. He had 200-plus yards in an overtime win (24–21 over the Oakland Raiders), and the heat and how he just got stronger and stronger and stronger as the game went on.

"We're back in here on Monday, watching the tape, grading it. It's still real hot outside, and Eddie was outside running 100s (100-yard dashes). Up and down, back and forth. That's Eddie George. You knew he was gonna be there every single week."

George would go the full 60 minutes until the final whistle. He was like a prizefighter whose game plan always was a late-round knockout. He'd take a defense's best shot and just keep coming.

"What sticks out to me is Eddie was always a guy that wore you down," Titans tight end Frank Wycheck said. "He wasn't gonna go busting an 80-yarder in the first series. He was a Joe Frazier-type of fighter. You were gonna eat iron fists the whole game.

"To see when we would take over games and see safeties and linebackers shy away from putting a hat on him…that was something. They didn't want to hit Eddie. No one wanted a part of him. They'd try him early on. He'd pop up and jaw. But when we took over, those guys conveniently got blocked or ran around blocks. He was as dominant as they come. He was the Earl Campbell of that era."

The Campbell parallel is an interesting one. Same franchise, same workhorse type of back. Campbell was more explosive. George was more reliable. Each was the face of the franchise during his era. Each shouldered much of the offensive load, and both led their teams deep into the playoffs.

"He seems a lot like myself," said Campbell, who was elected to the Pro Football Hall of Fame in 1991. "I am very impressed with him and his work ethic."

George eventually supplanted Campbell as the team's all-time leading rusher. He finished with 10,009 yards to Campbell's 8,574.

> **What sticks out to me is Eddie was always a guy that wore you down…You were gonna eat iron fists the whole game.**

"The biggest thing that impressed me about both of them was that they are both superstars of the NFL, but they never considered themselves in that light and there was always a great hunger to improve and get better," said lineman Bruce Matthews, the only man to be a teammate of both players. "It was a relentless pursuit of bettering themselves."

Eddie George quickly became the face of the Titans' franchise. (Photo courtesy Tennessee Titans)

Work ethic was key to Eddie George's success as a football player. (Photo courtesy Tennessee Titans)

George called it an honor to be mentioned in the same breath with Campbell. "(Earl) got to that level by running hard, by his passion to get it done, week in and week out," George said. "The man put his all into what he did. He played every play like it was his last play."

The thing about George that won over his teammates and coaches, besides his consistent performance, was his work ethic. He might have been a superstar, a perennial Pro Bowl back, but he always practiced and worked out as if he were a sixth-round pick fighting for a spot on the roster.

"He taught me how to be professional, how to work, how to play," Titans wide receiver Kevin Dyson said. "My rookie year, we're going through two-a-days. We were running 300-yard shuttles, two of them. I was in great shape. At least, I thought I was. I tried to keep up with Eddie. He was 240-something pounds to my 200 pounds. I ran with him in that first one, but I was hurting so bad. That second one I was like four people behind him. He almost lapped me. He was in such great shape. Man, that showed me this guy wants it. He had all the yardage and all the accolades, and he could care less about it. He would much rather have won the Super Bowl than rushed for 1,500 yards. That's always the person he was."

The Titans wouldn't have reached their one and only Super Bowl to date without George. Not only did he post 1,304 rushing yards and nine touchdowns during the 1999 regular season, but he was even better in the postseason. In the wild-card game against Buffalo, he rushed for 106 yards. In the divisional game at Indianapolis, he gained a franchise playoff-record 162 yards and had a touchdown. In the AFC Championship Game against Jacksonville, he pounded away for 86 yards. And against the St. Louis Rams in Super Bowl XXXIV, he rushed for a pair of touchdowns among his 28 carries for 95 yards.

The Rams prevailed, though, 23–16. It was a heartbreaking loss, but it sealed George's resolve to come back even bigger and better a year later.

"Wednesday after the parade and post wrapup meetings were all over with, Eddie came into my office," Fisher said. "He said, 'Coach, I don't want to go the Pro Bowl.' I said, 'Eddie, are you crazy? What are you talking about?' He had to get on a plane and go. He said, 'I don't want to go.' I said, 'Eddie, it's a chance to go and unwind and play with the best players in the league and be recognized.' And he said, 'Jeff, I want to get started on next season right now, here, today.' That was what the whole experience did for this organization. That was the attitude moving forward."

George burst from the gates in 2000 and never looked back. He rushed for a career-high 1,509 yards that season and made his fourth consecutive Pro Bowl. The Titans went 13–3 and were the top seed in the AFC for the playoffs. But George's great season ended in a thud at home against the Baltimore Ravens in a divisional playoff game.

The teams split the season series, with the Titans winning in Baltimore 14–6 in October and the Ravens returning the favor 24–23 in Nashville three weeks later. The Ravens knocked George out of the first meeting early in the first quarter with a sprained right knee. He carried only once, for 4 yards, but the Titans defense carried them to the victory. In the second matchup, the Ravens, the league's stoutest defense, held George to 28 yards on 12 carries. They were easily his two worst games of the season. In Tennessee's other 14 games, George piled up 1,477 yards.

The Titans were confident heading into the playoffs, knowing that any AFC team that wanted to reach the Super Bowl would have to come through Nashville. Tennessee dominated the playoff game against Baltimore statistically, but the Ravens made big plays, including two blocked field goals, to hang around. George scored on a 2-yard run on the opening drive to give the Titans a 7–0 lead. The game was tied at 10 heading into the fourth quarter, but it turned on the second blocked field goal. Baltimore's Anthony Mitchell returned Al Del Greco's 37-yard attempt 90 yards for the go-ahead score.

Whatever life the Titans had after that was unplugged by Ravens linebacker Ray Lewis. McNair tossed a ball in the flat to George, who bobbled it, then had it taken away by the Baltimore linebacker. Lewis returned the interception 50 yards for a touchdown, and the Ravens won 24–10.

They ended up winning the Super Bowl a few weeks later, a title the Titans believe just as easily could have been theirs. George ended up having off-season toe surgery and hearing chirps from the media that the Ravens, and Lewis in particular, were in his head.

Maybe it appeared that way. The Ravens reeled off five consecutive wins in the series, including both meetings in 2001 and the one in 2002. But returning from off-season toe surgery, George was not the same player in 2001. The surgery repaired a torn tendon that attached his big toe to his right foot. The injury affected every step, every stride, every cut.

"I had a surgically repaired toe that wasn't ready for what I was asking it to do," George said.

He didn't complain at all, but his 2001 numbers were markedly down from the first five years of his career. It was the only season he played for the Titans in which he didn't top the 1,000-yard mark.

"Eddie wasn't able to generate any power," Titans strength and conditioning coach Steve Watterson said. "He couldn't push because the muscle had been inactive for so long. He couldn't create any power."

George without power was like Superman without a cape.

"Eddie basically had to learn to run all over again," Fisher said. "He puts a lot of emphasis on his off-season workouts and when he wasn't able to get in the work that he was accustomed to, that affected him. He knew that he wasn't going into the season 100 percent, and that bothered him."

George got another crack at the Ravens in the playoffs following the 2003 season. The game took place in Baltimore, and the running back was jacked. Despite suffering a dislocated shoulder in the first half tackling Ravens safety Ed Reed after an interception, he kept going.

"I was real nervous for a minute," George said. "I didn't know exactly what happened. I was trying to get it back in while I was on the ground, but it was still dislocated."

The training staff popped the shoulder back in place. George then had it X-rayed, and once it was determined there were no bone chips or strained ligaments, the shoulder was placed in a harness and he returned for the second half.

He gained 44 of his 88 yards in the final 30 minutes. And he continually butted heads with Lewis, who had 17 tackles.

"It was like two trains colliding in the night," tight end Frank Wycheck said. "Those were big-time collisions."

George refused to be derailed that day. He took the best Lewis had to offer and kept barreling down the tracks. They even jawed at each other face to face after Lewis tackled him near the sideline and George popped up as if to say he would not be backing down.

The Titans prevailed, exorcising the ghost of the Ravens. And the running back held his head high. "I could have fed into everything that was being said, how (the Ravens) had my number and Ray was in my head," George said. "But I chose not to. I just chose to focus on the fact that this was an opportunity to go out and battle for something far greater than my personal pride."

George's heart and work ethic long will be an example for the Titans' franchise.

"Eddie had all of the plaques on the wall and the Heisman, but I'll never forget how hard he worked," Wycheck said. "I enjoyed playing with him. He was a beast. He changed games. He was the epitome of a leader."

> *It was like two trains colliding in the night. Those were big-time collisions.*

STEVE McNAIR

For all of the accolades, for all of the unbelievable scrambles, for all of the incredible passes, Steve McNair's storied career can be boiled down to one word: toughness.

There were weeks he could barely practice, yet he still played on Sunday. There were weeks where he didn't practice, yet he still played on Sunday. A 70-percent Steve McNair was better than 98 percent of the quarterbacks in the league anyway.

"He's by far one of the toughest players I've ever been around," Titans coach Jeff Fisher said. "He's one of the more competitive people you'll ever meet, quietly competitive. It doesn't matter what you're doing, he's gonna try to win.

"We played these handball games back against the wall between the (practice) bubble during the off-season four or five years ago. Steve had been traveling, he'd had off-season surgery, he was just working his way back in. But he went out there and won every game the first day he showed up."

Stories of McNair's toughness are legendary around these parts. The word "gamer" never will be more aptly applied than in the case of McNair. McNair played in dozens of games in which virtually no other quarterback would have put on a uniform, much less attempted to play. Against the Pittsburgh Steelers in 2000 McNair was sidelined with a bruised sternum, or so everyone thought. But when Steelers linebacker Jason Gildon knocked Neil O'Donnell out of the game with less than three minutes to play, McNair entered and promptly led the Titans down the field for the winning score. In 2001, a painful lower back forced him to stand for an entire flight to California, but he started the next night against Oakland in another Titans victory. In 2005 he got an epidural just to be able to practice.

Perhaps the game most remembered by his teammates came in 2002 at the Meadowlands against the New York Giants. McNair hadn't practiced all week because of a rib injury and a bad case of turf toe. In fact, the pain was so intense the quarterback hadn't even thrown on the side.

The Titans had a so-so 6–5 record at the time, and they were coming off a loss at Baltimore. They trailed the Indianapolis Colts by a game in the AFC South, and their season hung in the balance. The Giants were 6–5, too, and fighting for their playoff lives as well. McNair dressed and took the field early to try and warm up, see what his arm could do, what his ribs would allow. He made a few short tosses and was ready to head back to the locker room.

"I really didn't know if I was going to play or not," McNair said. But he hadn't gone to the locker room to tell Fisher he couldn't go. Instead, he took a pain-killing injection for his ribs, and the trainers cut a hole in the top of his shoe to make his toe more comfortable.

"It was a late-afternoon game, windy, tough conditions," Titans tight end Frank Wycheck said. "I remember Steve walking off the bus and it looked like he needed crutches. Going up to New Jersey, O'Donnell was saying, 'I'm gonna get a shot.' We got out there for warmups and I said to Steve, 'You all right?' He said, 'I'll be all right.' It was the one time I said there's no way. No way he could play. He found a way."

Indeed he did. McNair passed for 334 yards and three touchdowns as the Titans rallied to beat the Giants in overtime, 32–29. It was the start of a five-game winning streak to end the season that propelled the Titans into the playoffs. McNair ran in a two-point conversion to tie the game late. He was in such excruciating pain that he had to switch the football from his right hand to his left so he could raise it into the air in celebration. The pain-killing shot on the right side had worn off.

"I would say he's the toughest guy I've ever been around," Titans guard Zach Piller said. "I figure if I look up and he's still got two arms and two legs, he's going to find a way to play."

Titans offensive coordinator Mike Heimerdinger's favorite story about McNair's legendary toughness came later that same season in 2002, in the AFC Divisional Playoff Game against Pittsburgh at LP Field. "He dislocated a finger (on his throwing hand). We thought Neil was going to get ready to go and I looked down and his finger was sticking straight sideways," Heimerdinger said. "I said, 'Can you take a snap?' He said, 'I will.' I looked at him like he was crazy and went and got Neil. The next thing I feel a tap on my shoulder and he says, 'Give me the play.' He went back in after a play, took us down and that's when Joe (Nedney) kicked the field goal (to win the game). When I saw his finger, I was almost getting sick to my stomach, much less getting him to answer the bell."

It was all in a day's work for the 6'2", 230-pound Mississippi native. "I always want to play," McNair said. "If you're going to be a leader, you have to put it out on the field. I tried to do that."

His teammates had so much respect and admiration for McNair that his status as their leader was unquestioned. The quarterback also grew very close to Fisher. The coach had stuck his neck out when the Titans drafted McNair with the third overall pick in the 1995 draft. His numbers at Alcorn State were eye-popping, but they were built against suspect Division I-AA opponents. The young coach and the young QB grew together. McNair's rookie season was Fisher's first full season in charge. The coach had the luxury of bringing McNair along slowly, but eventually they both knew whose job it would be, and it's what both of them wanted.

The time came near the end of the 1996 season, when starter Chris Chandler was sidelined with an ankle injury. Once McNair took over, Fisher's confidence in him never wavered. There were some tough times, especially when the fans and media didn't understand how much pain McNair was playing through.

During the 1999 season, what turned out to be the best in franchise history and culminated with the team's only Super Bowl appearance, McNair missed five games with a ruptured disc in his lower back that required surgery. The Titans went 4–1 under O'Donnell, and some questioned if the job should be McNair's upon his return. The thought never crossed Fisher's mind. The guy wearing No. 9 would always be his No. 1.

"Early in his career after really difficult injuries, I worried whether he'd play," Fisher said. "But late in his career, I knew he was gonna play. The hardest thing later was the no-practice weeks and West Coast travel. But he found a way. He always found a way."

Sure enough, McNair returned to the lineup a week ahead of schedule in time for the Titans to knock off the then-unbeaten St. Louis Rams 24–21 on Halloween. They closed the regular season by winning eight of 10 games, including their final four, to enter the playoffs feeling good about their chances. They then proceeded to knock off Buffalo at home and Indianapolis and Jacksonville on the road to set up a rematch with the Rams in Super Bowl XXXIV.

McNair and the offense struggled in the first half against the Rams. The Titans fell behind 16–0 in the third quarter before the quarterback rallied his team. They tied the game at 16 midway through the fourth quarter, marking the largest deficit erased in Super Bowl history. McNair was making plays with his arm and his legs, and the Rams had no answers.

St. Louis took a 23–16 lead on a Kurt Warner bomb to Isaac Bruce, but there still was 1:54 left on the clock. Starting from their own 10 after a holding penalty on the kickoff,

Steve McNair's status as the leader of the Titans was unquestioned. (Photo courtesy Tennessee Titans)

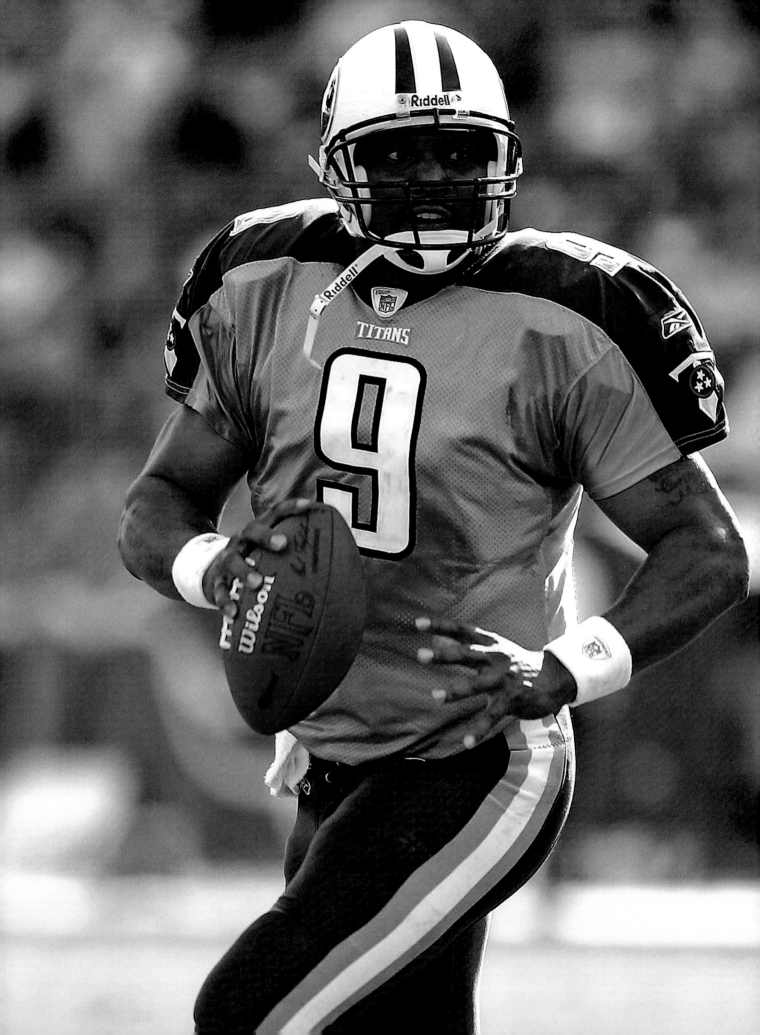

McNair methodically drove the Titans into Rams territory. Facing a third-and-five in the waning seconds, the Tennessee quarterback made a play that no other QB could have made to give his team a chance to win the game.

"No one can forget about the play when he stiff-armed Kevin Carter and escaped being sacked and threw a strike to (Kevin) Dyson for a first down to continue the drive," Titans running back Eddie George said. "Those plays, you are not going to see the Peyton Manning pretty pass to (Marvin) Harrison. What you are going to see is a man not wanting to go down and giving it his all, fighting for that last yard. We were amped off that. That was our inspiration."

Alas, the dream of a championship died hard on the next play, the game's final play. With six seconds to go from the Rams' 10, McNair correctly read the St. Louis coverage and fired to Dyson on a slant. Dyson had come in underneath Wycheck, who tried to clear out deep and take as many defenders with him as he could. Rams linebacker Mike Jones saw Dyson just before he turned his hips toward the end zone and was able to bring down the wide receiver less than yard from the potential game-tying touchdown.

"I don't ever want to feel like this again," said McNair, who had finished with 214 passing yards and 64 yards rushing, a Super Bowl record for a quarterback. "We were able to get some Super Bowl experience. When we come back the next time, we'll feel more comfortable. We're only going to get better."

The Titans have yet to make it back to a Super Bowl, but it was not for lack of effort and heart from McNair. "As he developed, so did the franchise," Fisher said. "He was instrumental in leading this franchise to its only Super Bowl appearance. He played in many games that no one else would have been able to play. He overcame an awful lot physically. He was there every week. He was a tremendous leader and set a great example for all the players that played with him. He was a great teammate. He is a good friend and personally I will always owe a lot to Steve. I grew as a coach through my experience with Steve."

The finest of McNair's hours with the Titans came in 2003, when he was named the league's co-MVP with Indianapolis Colts quarterback Peyton Manning. It was the culmination of years of hard work and dedication, of beating back stereotypes that he was an athlete playing quarterback and not just a great quarterback.

McNair was brilliant that season, ranking as the NFL's leading passer. He completed 62.5 percent of his attempts for 3,215 yards and a career-high 24 touchdowns. He had only seven interceptions, his lowest total since becoming the Titans' starter in 1997.

> **" What you are going to see is a man...giving it his all, fighting for that last yard. We were amped off that. That was our inspiration. "**

"In his MVP year he played most of the year hurt," running back Eddie George said. "It is a testament to his willingness to win and how he sacrificed his body for the team. We couldn't have won or been in the position had he not shown up. I know his attitude and determination permeated throughout the rest of the team and raised our level of play, because we said if our quarterback can come out here and play hurt, then we can suck it up and play hurt as well. That is where our mental toughness came from. It came from Steve McNair."

Steve McNair tucks the ball and runs for a first down against the Jacksonville Jaguars. (Photo courtesy Tennessee Titans)

McNair was moved by the recognition of the MVP award. He had harbored faint hopes of winning, fearing the two games he missed because of injury during the season would hinder his chances. The announcement came the day before an AFC Wild Card Playoff Game at Baltimore.

"Foremost I would like to thank the guys who paved the way for myself and a lot of other guys, the Warren Moons, the Doug Williams, the Randall Cunninghams," McNair said of his black quarterback predecessors. "This is something special; this is something I will cherish and take to my grave, that the things I accomplished will help others in the years to come."

McNair's tenure in Tennessee ended before the 2006 season. The franchise was in a difficult position with his contract, realizing the figure it had to pay him that season would have prevented it from signing its draft class. The Titans ultimately worked out a trade to send McNair to the Baltimore Ravens for a fourth-round draft pick.

"Steve would have loved to finish his career with the Titans," Titans offensive tackle Brad Hopkins said. "He still bleeds blue and red, we all know that. He made his mark in Tennessee. The Ravens got our leftovers. The Ravens should thank us for giving them a chance to have him for a little while. But we all know, even though he was wearing a Ravens helmet, we all know he probably had a Titans headband on underneath."

McNair announced his retirement from pro football on April 17, 2008. He said the wear and tear finally had taken too much of a toll.

"It was a hard decision, but I think it's a good decision," McNair said at his final news conference. "I'm always a team player first. Mentally, I could go out there and play. But physically, I just couldn't do it anymore—not to the capacity that I need to help my teammates win a football game."

McNair retired as one of only three quarterbacks in NFL history to throw for 30,000 yards and rush for 3,500 yards. The others, Fran Tarkenton and Steve Young, are in the Pro Football Hall of Fame.

"It's been a long road, but I've been fortunate to surround myself with great people, great coaches, great teammates, and great family," McNair said. "My career speaks for itself. I can reflect back on it and not change a thing. I played the game with a lot of passion and a lot of heart, and it showed over the course of my 13 years."

Everyone who wore the blue and red alongside him strongly agrees.

"He played through stuff not just most quarterbacks, but most players, wouldn't play through," Dyson said. "He sacrificed for us. I can't say enough about the guy for what he did for me. I've dropped balls and run poor routes and he never said anything bad about me and had enough faith in me to come back to me the next play or the play after that. So many quarterbacks, you see his reaction when a guy runs a wrong route and pouts or points at him and screams. You never saw Steve McNair do that."

Wycheck doesn't have a clue how his NFL career would have played out if not for his symbiotic relationship with McNair.

"He willed himself and his team to be great," the tight end said. "We followed his lead and his toughness.

"You can use all of the clichés, all of the descriptions of what you think a football player is, and that's Steve McNair. The hits that he took, the style he played, he took some big shots. But he was a bull out there, a raging bull. He'd take shots like a fullback, take the snap, run around and do it again. He always came through."

The guys who may have loved McNair the most were his linemen. Hall of Famer Bruce Matthews and tackle Brad Hopkins blocked for McNair the entirety of his career with the Titans. "The thing I liked about Steve was he really didn't care what his stats were, it was really all about winning," Matthews said. "He could care less about where he stood in the league. Plus, he always made you look good if your guy got by you in pass protection, because he'd make guys miss."

Not that a lot of guys were getting past Matthews and Hopkins. But they saw McNair as one of their own, something linemen don't often believe about their quarterback. "He had that lineman-type mentality where it wasn't about the notoriety or fame," Matthews said. "It was just to compete for the sake of competing, whether it was playing football or throwing a wad of paper into the waste-paper basket. He was the ultimate competitor."

> *The hits that he took, the style he played, he took some big shots. But he was a bull out there, a raging bull.*

The Titans probably will consider retiring McNair's jersey. "People will remember Steve in different lights," Hopkins said. "To me, he will always be my little brother. I would do anything for him. I have seen his career from the day he got drafted until now. He will always be my quarterback."

FRANK WYCHECK

In professional wrestling, a good guy is known as a "face," short for babyface. The bad guy is known as a "heel." The fans love to cheer for the faces. That's the way the promoters draw it up.

Frank Wycheck, a self-professed wrestling fan who climbed into the ring and had a match at TNA Wrestling's "Slammiversary" pay-per-view event in Nashville after his football career was over, is perhaps the biggest "face" in Titans franchise history. The tight end was their Everyman, a guy who lucked into the right situation and turned it into gold.

Wycheck played at the University of Maryland, and when he left he was the Terrapins' all-time leader in receptions with 134. His best season in College Park may have been his first, when he established a school record with 58 receptions.

Still, he was largely overlooked during the 1993 NFL Draft. He eventually was taken in the sixth round by the Washington Redskins, 160th overall. Wycheck played two non-descript seasons in the nation's capital, appearing in just 18 games and making eight starts. His numbers were altogether modest: 23 receptions for 168 yards and one touchdown.

The Redskins had a glut of tight ends heading into the 1995 season, or so then-Redskins head coach Norv Turner believed. So when his team came to Tennessee to practice against the then-Houston Oilers at Maryville College, Turner had a chat with Oilers first-year head coach Jeff Fisher about Wycheck. Turner had been assistant coach at the University of Southern California while Fisher was a player there.

"(Former University of Tennessee star quarterback) Heath Shuler was their (the Redskins') quarterback and we were going to practice during the week and then play against them at the University of Tennessee in a preseason game," Fisher said. "Norv said

he knew we were looking for tight ends because we were a run-and-shoot team the year before. We didn't have tight ends. He said, 'I've got a fullback/tight end I'll give you for a six or seven because I don't think he's gonna make it.' That usually means they're gonna cut him, and they did and we claimed him."

It turned out to be a great move for the Titans and for Wycheck. He arrived with the Oilers just as the news was breaking that they were looking into a move to Nashville. It also was the rookie season of quarterback Steve McNair. Fortune couldn't have smiled any brighter on the burly Philadelphia native.

"It's kind of weird," Wycheck said. "I hit the right place at the right time. Steve was a young quarterback and the offense was in a state of transition to a whole different style. Jeff Fisher wanted to control the ball, move the chains and play hard-nosed defense. It fit me."

It sure did. No one, not even Wycheck, could have imagined how well. He started 10 games in his first season with the Oilers and had 40 receptions for 471 yards and a touchdown. The numbers might have seemed modest, but 11.8 yards per catch for a tight end was well above average. It meant Wycheck was moving the chains with nearly every catch, just as he said he would.

"For Frank it was all about opportunity," former Titans wide receiver Kevin Dyson said. "They had guys in Washington making more money, more established. He developed a little bit later. He got the chance in Houston. They needed tight ends. He got the opportunity, and he seized the moment."

And that was before McNair became the starter. He attempted only 80 passes in his rookie season, but he and Wycheck were beginning to develop a chemistry in practice that would lead to bigger and better things for both of them.

Beginning in 1996, Wycheck started all but one game over the course of the next seven seasons. And for most of those games, the guy pulling the trigger was McNair. They were a late '90s version of Joe Montana-to-Brent Jones.

"He and Steve had this rare connection," Fisher said. "Frank would be running one way and Steve would be running for his life and he'd throw the ball behind him and Frank would not see the ball thrown and just turn back around and catch the ball. It didn't just happen once. It was the relationship they had on the field.

"He was really our first tight end in the modern era. He was deserving of the [three] Pro Bowl appearances. He was fourth all-time in catches for tight ends. It speaks pretty well for a guy who was cut."

Wycheck was a perfect complement to an offense that featured McNair and running back Eddie George.

"When Les Steckel was the offensive coordinator it was like playing basketball on grass," Wycheck said. "It was, 'Get away from your guy, and Steve will find you.' Steve was unpredictable and we had an eye for finding each other."

Wycheck had at least 60 catches for five consecutive seasons starting in 1997. His three Pro Bowl trips came in consecutive seasons starting in 1998, when he had a career-high 70 receptions. He tied the mark in the 2000 season.

It's a funny thing, isn't it, that he will be best remembered outside of Nashville for throwing a pass instead of catching one? Technically, of course, it was a lateral, but it still was a spiraling thing of beauty, his toss to Kevin Dyson that set in motion the Music City Miracle.

Frank Wycheck looks for yardage during the 2003 AFC Championship Game against the Oakland Raiders. (Photo by Stephen Dunn/Getty Images)

Frank Wycheck reaches out to make a catch during the AFC Wildcard Playoff victory over the Buffalo Bills on January 8, 2000. (Photo by Allen Kee/NFL/Getty Images)

"I never just put on the tape and watch it," Wycheck said. "It comes up around playoff time every year. I'm definitely reminded of it wild-card weekend. It's on every list of top plays. I still…it's not like I'm tired of it. I love it. It brings back great memories, feelings of euphoria. It brings me back to a great time for me and for the franchise."

And what of his status as the Titans' Everyman? He knows he has found a niche in Nashville and will be a beloved figure in the Music City in perpetuity, though he's far too modest to admit it. Isn't that what makes him Everyman?

"I don't know what it is," said Wycheck, who joined play-by-play man Mike Keith in the booth for the Titans Radio Network in 2005. "I guess it's a guy fans look at and say, 'He did it, I could do it.' I wasn't flashy or the prettiest player out there like you see these days. People respected that I showed up and didn't talk much and did my job."

A number of concussions ultimately contributed to Wycheck's decision to retire after the 2003 season at the age of 32. He hung up his cleats with no regrets.

"I did everything I set out to do and much more," Wycheck said. "From a guy who wasn't even supposed to be in a training camp, let alone to where I ended up, I'm truly proud and I couldn't ask for anything more. It's been a truly great ride."

One in which almost every Titans fan felt like he or she was riding shotgun. They all enjoyed the ride, too.

KEITH BULLUCK

Nobody likes losing. Some people, though, handle it better than others.

Keith Bulluck is decidedly not one of them. It really grates on him, but you have to consider his background and the timing of his arrival with the Tennessee Titans. Bulluck, a linebacker out of Syracuse, was the first-round pick of the AFC Champion Titans in 2000, No. 30 overall. He came to a team that had gone 13–3 and been within a foot, perhaps, of winning the Super Bowl.

He played at Syracuse when the Orange was pretty good, too. It went to three consecutive bowl games while Bulluck was a starter, including a Fiesta Bowl and an Orange Bowl.

The Titans posted another 13–3 record the year Bulluck arrived. He was used primarily as a backup because the team was set at linebacker with Eddie Robinson, Randall Godfrey, and Greg Favors, but that was OK because he was in a veteran locker room and he was afforded time to learn the game.

The Titans stumbled to a 7–9 mark in 2001, but they bounced back to go 11–5 in 2002 and 12–4 in 2003. Bulluck had become not only a starter, but one of the team's better players. He was part of a winning formula, and he had grown accustomed to it. When the Titans took a two-year downturn after the 2003 season, Bulluck seethed.

"He's very competitive," Titans coach Jeff Fisher said. "He does not like losing. He had a difficult time when we dipped for a year or two, but he trusted that we'd get back."

The fact is, Bulluck says, he simply didn't know how to react.

"I was accustomed to winning and it just got to a point where…the rebuilding process, it's different between the NFL and college," Bulluck said. "In college you're there four-five years and everybody moves on. In the NFL you're there four, five, six, seven years and if you don't move on, other people move on. They guys you are used to playing with are gone and new guys are coming in. You're on the same team, but it's a different team because the faces are changing.

"It was a tough time. We had a lot of youth, a lot of guys that had to play who wouldn't necessarily have been playing. It was very frustrating for me. I asked the question: 'What are we gonna do to get better?' I don't know where that took everything, but I definitely didn't want the losing ways to continue."

When Bulluck says he asked the question, he means that he asked it publicly. He was trying to step into the leadership role, but perhaps not in the best way imaginable. His

comments sometimes upset the front office at Baptist Sports Park's team headquarters. Fisher realized it was just the linebacker's way.

"He sees us back now, though," Fisher said. "And he's in the prime of his career. He's got a lot of years and a lot of plays left. He has been kind of a fixture since those days. He's one of the few players that got to enjoy and experience the ride and the good teams and unfortunately experience the downside, but he hung in and rode it out."

He rode it out, but he readily admits to hitting a few potholes.

"At first it was weird (taking a leadership role). I was always making sure I was taking care of doing my job," Bulluck said. "I was always the younger guy. Eddie Robinson was in my room (Robinson played linebacker for the Titans from 1998-2001). He was like a 10-year guy and I was a rookie.

"When it was my time was when we had our decline and lull. It was tough day in and day out knowing I had to put a right face on and do the right things. To be honest it was real tough. I was maybe not always the best leader. But at end of day you don't ask to be a leader, people appoint you. You just lead the best you know how."

The coach never has been able to argue with Bulluck's production. The 6'3", 235-pounder is a tackling machine, leading the Titans in that department for five consecutive seasons from 2002-06. He entered the 2008 season on a string of 113 consecutive starts. He led the team in interceptions in 2007 with five. He made the Pro Bowl in 2003.

In an age where sack specialists and run-stuffers are coming and going from the field as though on line shifts in a hockey game, Bulluck truly is an anomaly. He's an every-down linebacker who can sack the quarterback (17.5 career sacks), stuff the run (1,027 career tackles), and drop and cover (16 career interceptions).

The problem is he has gone largely unnoticed in his career. Whether it's because of Nashville's small market size relative to other NFL cities or because his sack numbers aren't as gaudy as some others at his position, one Pro Bowl amounts to more of a slap in the face than a reward.

"He's underrated," Fisher said. "He plays at a Pro Bowl level every year. Unfortunately at his position the guys who get voted in at outside linebacker are pass-rushers and sack specialists, not true linebackers, and that's what Keith is."

Bulluck has gotten over the lack of personal recognition. Does it put a chip on his shoulder? Absolutely. "Most definitely I've been overlooked," Bulluck said. "I'm going into my ninth year [in 2008]. Personally I've done anything you could do in this league except win Defensive MVP and a Super Bowl. I've been to Pro Bowls, been All-Pro. I've been overlooked, but I stopped thinking about it 2–3 years ago. There's nothing I can do about the politics of the league or the market we're in. I don't work any less hard, and I go out week in and week out to prove I am one of the best players at my position. As long as I'm healthy and I'm given the opportunity, that's my goal, to be the best I can be."

In many ways, Bulluck is the one player who has bridged the gap between the 1999 Super Bowl team led by Steve McNair and Eddie George to the 2007 playoff team led by a stingy defense and quarterback Vince Young. No, he didn't play on the Super Bowl team, but he came in the following year. He joined a team full of leaders. There were guys in the locker room such as Eddie Robinson, Blaine Bishop, McNair, and George.

"I learned a lot from those guys," Bulluck said. "The player I am definitely comes from me wanting to play however I play, but I got a lot from those guys. I learned what the

In an age of specialists, Keith Bulluck proved himself to be a throwback every-down linebacker. (Photo by Paul Spinelli/Getty Images)

Keith Bulluck brings down Brian Westbrook of the Philadelphia Eagles during a 2006 game. (Photo by Tom Briglia/NFL/Getty Images)

league was about, how to be a professional, how to be a vet. I saw how those guys went about their business. I learned how to be a student of the game. Coming out of college I was big into film, but those guys helped me become even more of a student."

Despite playing on the other side of the ball, George was of particular inspiration to Bulluck. Bulluck had been a running back in high school in addition to playing defense. He was a tall, upright runner who did a lot of damage between the tackles, not unlike a player he watched win the Heisman Trophy at Ohio State.

"Eddie was the ultimate pro," Bulluck said. "I wish he was around to show these guys what it's like to be a professional. No matter how much teams pounded on him, he was out there on Monday. He didn't like to come off the field. I used to look up to him. He represented this organization. He was what a leader is supposed to be."

The only players on the Titans roster from the Super Bowl team are defensive end Jevon Kearse, who is back in 2008 after a four-year stint with the Philadelphia Eagles, and punter Craig Hentrich. No one else has been around the franchise as long as Bulluck.

"It's cool just to have another familiar face, someone you've been to war with, someone you know has your back, someone you know what you're gonna get from him. I think Jevon is gonna prove a lot of people wrong, that he's not near the end of his career," Bulluck said. "It's tough to rush the passer when you're head-up on the tight end.

"We're gonna give people hell this year with Kyle (Vanden Bosch) on one side and Jevon on the other and Albert in the middle. That's a hell of a D-line. I'm preparing myself this off-season to have the best season of my career, definitely."

> **There's nothing I can do about the politics of the league or the market we're in. I don't work any less hard, and I go out week in and week out to prove I am one of the best players at my position.**

Sounds like something a leader would say. Sounds like something George would be proud of.

Definitely.

BRUCE MATTHEWS

The first rule of Bruce Matthews is that he does not talk much about Bruce Matthews.

The second rule of Bruce Matthews is that he does not talk much about Bruce Matthews.

Fortunately, he doesn't have to. His play during 19 seasons in the NFL, all with the same organization, speaks volumes for him. You'll find his bust in Canton, the first Tennessee Titan to be elected to the Pro Football Hall of Fame. His career spanned 14 seasons with the Houston Oilers and five with the franchise after it moved to the Volunteer State. He started 229 consecutive games along the offensive line, and he played in 296, more games than any non-kicker in NFL history. He made a record-tying 14 consecutive Pro Bowls.

Matthews was 6'5", 305 pounds with hands like sides of beef. He had good feet and a great feel for the game. Because of that, his versatility was unmatched in the annals of the game. He is the only lineman in the Hall of Fame who played significant time at all five positions. He made 17 starts at left tackle, 22 at right tackle, 67 at right guard, 87 at center, and 99 at left guard. The question wasn't whether to put him in the Hall, but at what position? You can check the Pro Football Hall of Fame's website; Matthews is the only lineman in the modern era without a position next to his name. When you call up his bio it says: "Position: Guard-Tackle-Center."

What a luxury for a coach, having a guy he could plug into any hole on the line and know he was going to get high-caliber play. Matthews also knew every trick in the book.

He probably wrote a chapter or two himself. "He would say he'd get a young guy chirping on a play, and Bruce would be like, 'Listen, kid, you never even pissed a drop in this league, don't be talking.' Then he'd beat him like a drum the next play," former Titans tight end Frank Wycheck said.

When Jeff Fisher arrived with the Oilers and became the head coach shortly thereafter, Matthews already had been with the franchise for 11 years. But they knew each other. Matthews also played at the University of Southern California, where Fisher had played. Their years with the Trojans under John Robinson overlapped for a couple of seasons before Fisher was taken by the Chicago Bears in the seventh round of the 1981 NFL Draft. Matthews would be taken in the first round by the Oilers in 1983.

"I knew he'd be a great player," Fisher said. "I watched him get drafted, watched him play. When I came in here in 1994, he played all of these positions along the line. He was a tremendous athlete. He just knew how to survive inside.

"He was so smart and so physically talented, but the thing that motivated Bruce and motivates all great players was fear of failure. He didn't want to fail. It motivated him year after year to maintain that conditioning level and that edge in the game. To play as many games as consistently as he did and to be a first-ballot Hall of Famer speaks for itself."

His presence was a constant. He was a quiet role model for every Titan who followed. "He was my favorite player of all time," Wycheck said. "I looked up to him. I was in awe of him. I'm proud to be able to say he was my friend. He was a great role model. You wanted to turn out to be him.

"What I respected the most about him, we'd talk about the Hall of Fame and he wouldn't talk about it. He hated that stuff. But to be a small part of his career…I felt good about it to see him go in. To play with him and listen to him and watch how he went about things was just awesome. He's the ultimate guy. He had fun, he was competitive, a great family guy, a great dad. Every nice thing you can say about someone, that's Bruce."

He also was a bit of an instigator. That's why you have to watch the quiet guy in the back of the room with the wry grin. In the back of the Titans locker room, chances are that guy was Matthews. When the Oilers moved to Nashville in 1997 and held training camp at Tennessee State University, several players rented golf carts to get around campus and conserve energy. Matthews took to hiding them or rigging them so they wouldn't run.

"Whenever anything funny was up, Bruce was in the background smiling," Fisher said. "He was the first one on the practice field, and the last one off. It wasn't because he was doing extra work; it was because he was playing some kind of game. He always had to be competing. They'd be throwing footballs at helmets or some other kind of game that he made up, and he always won."

Matthews created a variety of games to keep himself amused on the practice field and in the locker room. The linemen would make human pyramids before practices. "Bucket Ball" was played in the locker room as players tried to toss a football into a laundry cart at the end of the room. Matthews was all-time quarterback during Saturday practices, when offensive linemen would run pass routes. When he retired after 19 years, most of the shenanigans went with him.

"I think everyone has a little Bruce in him," former Titans offensive tackle Fred Miller said. "Bruce brought so much to the table that you just can't put your finger on one thing. It was the whole attitude and atmosphere."

Matthews called it a career six months after the 2001 season. He had ended his career on the 229-game starting streak. He hadn't told anyone he had planned on retiring, but

Bruce Matthews, shown here playing center, ended his career with a string of 229 straight starts. At various times, he started at all five positions on the offensive line. (Andy Lyons/Allsport/Getty Images)

he played his last game on Jan. 6, 2002, against the Cincinnati Bengals. Despite starting, Matthews was in for only four plays. His final offensive play was a 41-yard touchdown pass from Steve McNair to Derrick Mason. "I thought, 'If that is my last play, then that's a pretty good way to go out," Matthews said.

Less than a year later, on Dec. 8, 2002, the Titans welcomed Matthews back to town for a formal ceremony. The team retired his jersey No. 74 at halftime of a game against the Colts. "I came to the Oilers and at my first press conference they held up 74," Matthews said. "I said, 'Man, that's a big slug number.'

"I grew into it over the years."

Now it's too big for anyone else.

BRUCE MATTHEWS' HALL OF FAME ENSHRINEMENT

The most anyone in Nashville had ever heard Bruce Matthews speak was at his induction ceremony into the Pro Football Hall of Fame on Aug. 5, 2007. Here is the complete transcript of his induction, including his speech and the speech by his presenter, Mike Munchak, a former teammate, current Titans offensive line coach, and fellow Hall of Famer:

Mike Munchak, presenter

I first met Bruce Matthews in training camp in 1983. He was the first-round draft choice that season and I was entering my second year with the Houston Oilers. It was his first training camp practice, so obviously all eyes were on him. He didn't disappoint. He came off the ball with such quickness, got into his blocks, great finish, great work ethic. He was amazing.

His footwork, now, wasn't. His footwork was something to watch. His feet were all over the place. He was like a human weed whacker.

Despite that, we knew that he was going to be something special. From that first practice in training camp, I think the coaches quickly realized that because of Bruce's intelligence and his athletic ability, he was capable of playing many positions along the offensive line. His first five years in the league they moved him around quite a bit.

In 1988, his sixth season, he settled down, moved inside to the guard and center spot, which gave him a chance to master one position. He responded with 14 Pro Bowls in a row, made All-Pro at center and guard numerous times, went on to be a great player for us. He not only played the five positions inside, he was our snapper on field goals and PATs. He snapped on the punts, which meant he had to cover.

That was some good comedy there, watching him cover a kick. He was our emergency quarterback. If a couple quarterbacks ever went down, he on occasion would get a snap in practice. He was also our backup kicker. He worked on kickoffs, punts. Wasn't a great kicker by any means, but that's the kind of value he had to our team, that we felt he could fit in all those spots if need be during a game.

Once he got up in the 200s, I think people started bringing [the consecutive games started streak] to his attention. It was nothing he ever dwelled on or he felt was a defining moment for him or his career. I think it was something he was looking at now after he retired wondering, How did I ever do that?

I acquired a whole new respect for him when I became his coach. So having a guy like Bruce as versatile as he was for me that I can move him around, as a coach, I slept well at night knowing I had a guy like him that could do those kind of things for me.

He played during three different decades. He played over 300 games, including playoffs. He didn't miss one game because of injury. You knew somehow he was going to be able to line up on Sunday, and he always did. I think he's the kind of guy that could have played in any era. For 19 years, he was as good as anyone that's ever played the game. His accomplishments speak for themselves.

I don't know if there's ever been another player like Bruce Matthews in the NFL, and I don't know if there will ever be another one again. Bruce and I have a unique relationship. I was his teammate for 11 years, his coach for eight years, but more importantly he has been like family to me for the past 24 years.

We played together on the offensive line for the Houston Oilers for more than a decade. I played left guard. As you saw in the videotape, he played everywhere else. His work ethic, his competitiveness, his passion for the game, were contagious. I know that he motivated me to become a better player. Many of his former teammates, several who are here today, would say the same.

He raised the standard for all of us. Competitive is the word that best describes Bruce. His desire to be the best is unmatched. He wants to win at everything he does: a sport, a video game, even an argument. He can claim an opinion he doesn't even believe in just to see if he can still win the argument.

Classic Bruce, though, is when you're in a car with him and a song comes on the radio. He immediately yells out the name of the song and the artist. He would say, "Springsteen, Glory Days, bam." Even though no one else is playing this game, he's still competing. But the games that Bruce made up in the locker room are legendary and are still being played today. Ball Master, Helmet Ball, Monkey in the Middle were some of his creations. Of course, the rules are made up by him to facilitate his winning. Over the years he involved many of his teammates in these locker room games. They definitely helped to build camaraderie, relax the players, and ultimately may have contributed to improving their play on Sundays.

I think that Bruce's competitive spirit was his secret weapon and a reason why he played 19 seasons. It kept him young at heart. He always found a way to make it fun, and it showed on the field every Sunday.

When I retired from playing I contemplated going into coaching. One of the motivating factors for me was having the opportunity to coach Bruce and to continue our football relationship. This could be potentially a tough thing, coaching your best friend. But Bruce made it easy for me, I think because I let him do whatever he wanted to do. But he was always a professional through and through. I took advantage of his leadership and experience and let him show the other linemen through his work habits what it took to be a pro. It was obviously an honor to coach him.

Bruce and I have followed parallel paths during our days in the NFL. We were drafted a year apart by the Houston Oilers in the first round. As offensive linemen, we had similar successes on the field. We shared sweet victories and unfortunately some tough losses. We have been business partners. We were married two weeks apart. Our wives, Marci and Carrie of 24 years, became best of friends, and our children are like brothers and sisters.

Because of our similar experiences, we developed a special bond that goes way beyond the football field. There were many nights after we put our kids to bed that we'd get together and talk for hours. Sometimes we would just sit outside on Bruce's ranch and have a beer, other times we'd go bowling or play some one-on-one basketball, which I guess I'll admit he usually won. But during this time together, we'd have great discussions about our careers, our families and our Christian walks. We were always there to encourage or challenge each other as we worked our ways through life's ups and downs.

Now that Bruce is retired from the NFL, these talks have continued over the phone lines. Bruce, I just want you to know I've always appreciated your advice and honesty over the years. You've been a great example to me of what it takes to be a good husband, father, and Christian. I'm blessed to know you.

It's hard to believe that Bruce has played in 296 regular season games, more than any other player, excluding kickers, in NFL history. During a 19-year career, he never missed a game due to injury. He has played approximately 18,000 plays. As his teammate and coach,

I have seen every snap Bruce has taken in the NFL. So I know that I'm qualified to stand here today and proudly say, over there sits Bruce Matthews, one of the best to ever play the game.

Bruce, you should be proud. You took the talent that God gave you and used it to the best of your ability. Job well done. Let me be the first to officially welcome you into the Pro Football Hall of Fame family. It is my privilege to present you for enshrinement into the Pro Football Hall of Fame, Bruce Matthews.

Bruce Matthews

I'd first like to say how honored and blessed I am to be here. If someone had told me when I was a kid that one day I would play in the NFL…let alone be inducted in the Pro Football Hall of Fame, I wouldn't have believed them. I consider it an honor and a privilege to be standing up here today, and I'd like to thank the Lord Jesus Christ for blessing me and my family so much.

As much as I'd like to take credit for everything that's happened in my career, I know it was only because of how the Lord blessed me that I was able to accomplish what I did. My part was the easy part: just go out and use the talents and abilities God gave me. God blessed me with the size, the desire to play the game. He kept me injury free and brought many wonderful coaches and players into my life, and for this I'm very thankful.

Let me begin by thanking the Pro Football Hall of Fame and everyone that has been involved in this week. My wife Carrie and I are amazed at the treatment my family has received since we were named in February. It's added to our enjoyment of this weekend. I'd also like to offer my congratulations to my fellow Hall of Fame classmen. Getting to know them and their families has been a great part of this weekend.

I'd like to thank John McClain of the *Houston Chronicle* and David Climer of *The Tennessean* for all they did in getting me elected. I believe that John McClain is one of the most knowledgeable football reporters around, and I'm thankful for his friendship over the last 25 years.

I'd like to thank the owner of the Tennessee Titans, Mr. Bud Adams, for all he did for me and my family in Houston and then in Nashville. I'd like to thank Mike Halovak, Lad Herzog and Ed Bowls for drafting me back in the day.

There have been so many great people in the Oilers/Titans organization over the years, and I'd like to thank them all. But I'd especially like to thank Gordon "Red" Batty, Paul "Hoss" Noska, the late Bill "Mojo" Lackey for taking care of me in the equipment room.

I was blessed to play 19 years and never miss a game due to injury, but I had a lot of help from the trainers, especially Brad Brown, Don Moseley and Geoff Kaplan. I'd like to thank my strength and conditioning coach, Steve Watterson, for his expertise and especially his friendship.

One of my favorite parts of game week was drinking coffee and joking with our head of security, Joe Dugger, who passed away a couple years ago, the night before the game, after the team meal had cleared. There are so many memories. I'm thankful for all of them.

I grew up in a very athletic family, the youngest of five children. We were very close. My parents, Daisy and Clay Matthews, set an example of excellence, honesty, integrity, and love for which I feel very blessed. Although my mother Daisy passed away after my rookie season in 1984, I owe so much to the love and support she gave me and all us kids while growing up, and I miss her very much.

I'm thankful for my older sister, Christie, and all the support and love she's given me and how she never let me get too full of myself. I love you. My older twin brothers Brad and Raymond were always an inspiration to me in how they competed in the Special Olympics. Although Brad passed away in 2002, they've always been my biggest supporters and I love them very much. I love you, Ray.

Many people never had anyone that they looked up to while they were growing up, but I was blessed to have two people in my house who were my role models. The first was my father, Clay Sr. He is without a doubt the man I most admire and respect in this world. He played in the early 1950s for the San Francisco 49ers. Although I never saw him play, I can only imagine he would have been a handful to play against. My dad taught me about doing what was right no matter what the cost, never quitting, and what it meant to be a man of integrity.

One of my finest memories of the day the Hall of Fame results were announced was three or four hours later after the phone lines had cleared and I finally had a chance to talk to my dad. I said, 'Dad, did you hear the news?' My dad jokingly said, 'Yeah, I didn't make it in again. I guess I'm no longer eligible (laughter).' Obviously we had a great laugh, and I just want to say, Pop, I love you very much. I still respect and admire you.

My next role model was my older brother Clay. Cleveland Brown. He is five years older than me. So as I grew up, he was the one I wanted to be like. He was and still is my favorite player of all time. I love to brag to teammates about him. He played linebacker for the Cleveland Browns for 16 years and the Atlanta Falcons for three years. Since the Browns were a division rival of the Oilers, I got to play against him 23 times. Getting to play against your idol twice a year was one of the highlights of my career, and it was always something I looked forward to. I especially loved to play in Cleveland and check out all the banners and No. 57 jerseys in the crowd, see how much they loved him and still do.

I always felt as though I was witnessing something special, something that nobody else had had the opportunity to do in the history of the game. My favorite part of game week was Wednesday morning, when our offensive coordinator would give an overview of the Browns defense. I would beam with pride as he talked about how we would deal with my brother. I had to learn to watch every play on film twice: First time I watched my brother, and then the second time I had to watch the guy who I was supposed to block.

My hope was that my brother would have a great game individually, but we would win the game. Although it ended up pretty even. One of us won 12 and one of us won 11. As many times as I counted, I can't remember who won the most. Those games proved challenging and I would find my mind wandering, wondering how my brother was doing. It took me a couple of years to learn how to prepare and play against him. In 1986, he beat me for a sack. Although I hated giving up sacks, I didn't mind because it was to him, although I swore not to let it happen again, and it didn't (laughter).

I want to go on the record as saying that my brother Clay Matthews was without a doubt the best all around linebacker I've ever played with or against. There were some who may have been better at one discipline of linebacking, but none better all-around. He played outside, inside, played the run well, covered backs, wide receivers, tight ends, rushed the passer, and excelled at all of them. In an era of specialization, he was on the field every play and holds the record for most games played by a linebacker. The only negative surrounding my induction into the Hall of Fame is that my brother isn't already in here.

All I can say is I look forward to the day when he's standing up here getting inducted because he's very deserving. He taught me about hard work, discipline, dedication, and the mindset necessary to excel. He was not only a role model, a big brother, but a best friend, and I thank God for him. I love you, my brother.

I've been blessed over the years with many great coaches and players that I've had the opportunity to work with. I'd like to thank my high school coach, Dick Sauder, from Arcadia, California, who made it here today. Thanks, coach. And my line coaches, Bob Digiacomo and Paul Weinberger, for working with me as well. I've been amazed by the support of my former Apache teammates. I want to thank them for being here today and at the event in California last month. I must also make a special recognition of my best friend from high school, Big Dave Sam Samarsachic for being such a great friend and keeping the Apache spirit alive.

Playing football at the University of Southern California was one of the greatest experiences of my life, and I'd like to thank my head coach, John Robinson, who is here today, and my line coaches, my offensive line coaches, Hudson Hauck and Jerry Ataway for all they did for me. Playing with future Hall of Famers Anthony Munoz, Ronnie Lott, Marcus Allen, and my future head coach, Jeff Fisher, and numerous No. 1 draft choices taught me how to compete and made me a better player. At this time also I take great pride in the fact that USC has the most players in the Pro Football Hall of Fame.

I'd especially like to thank my former teammates, Don Mosebar and Dave Holden, and my roommate from college, Doug Branscom, for their friendship and for putting up with me. Getting drafted by the Houston Oilers was a dream come true. I have many great memories from the good years as well as the not-so-good ones. I want to thank the fans of Houston for all their support and love they showed me and say that there was nothing like the Astrodome on a Sunday afternoon.

When the team moved in 1997, it was a big shock to me, but it really turned out to be a blessing. I want to thank the fans of Tennessee for the five great years that I spent in Nashville. I also want to thank my buddy Bob Queen for working out with me in Texas for so many years when the team moved up to Tennessee and I still stayed in Texas in the off-season, especially as we were approaching 40 years old. Thanks, Bob.

I was blessed to play with so many great players and coaches over my 19 years, but I'd love to thank them all personally. I'd like to thank the team chaplains, who gave me so much spiritual support and helped me stay grounded in my faith. I'd like to thank Greg Headington for leading me to the Lord, Mike Meyers, James Mitchell, and Reggie Pleasant. I'd like to recognize and thank my offensive line coaches, Bill Walsh, who is here today, Kim Helton, the late Bob Young, Larry Bechtol, Renney Simmons and Mike Munchak.

Mike Munchak was my teammate for 11 years. He was my roommate in the hotel and the offensive lineman that I aspired to be like. He was my best friend, my advisor and an example of the man I wanted to be like. His family and mine are very close. We love Marci, Alex and Julie very much. As great as a player as Mike was, a Hall of Famer obviously, I believe that Mike is an even better coach. Mike was able to communicate to his players like no coach I had ever had, and I believe that he helped me become a better player each of the eight seasons that he coached me. Introducing Mike for his induction in the Hall of Fame in 2001 was one of the biggest thrills of my life. I'm honored that he introduced me today. I thank God for my friendship with Mike. You're like a brother to me and I love you very much.

God has blessed me with a wonderful wife and family. So much of my success is due to the support and love they have given me. We've been blessed with seven children: Steven, Kevin, Marilyn, Jake, Mikey, Luke and Gwinny. You're each a gift from God and I love you all very much.

I met my wife Carrie at USC. She is the one thing that I cherish most on this earth. You are my best friend, and I hate to think what life would be without you. As great as all the athletic awards and accolades have been, they do not compare to knowing and loving you. I thank God for you and I look forward to whatever He has in store for us next. Thank you for making these last 27 years so awesome. I love you very much.

In conclusion, I want to say that having your name mentioned with the all-time greats of the game is a tremendous honor and very humbling to me. It is a dream come true, and I'd like to thank everyone, once again, who had anything to do with getting me here. I've never been more aware of how much the Lord Jesus Christ has blessed me and loves me than at this very moment, and I want to thank Him again because that is where the credit is due. Thank you all for this amazing honor. Thank you.

JEVON KEARSE

Contrary to popular belief, Jevon Kearse never has leaped a tall building in a single bound. Maybe a medium building.

Tales of the defensive end's athletic ability are legendary. Then again, they should be. If you're going to maintain the nickname "The Freak" in the NFL, where 230-pound linebackers are running 4.4-second 40-yard dashes and offensive linemen are bench-pressing, well, medium buildings, you had better be otherworldly.

"When we drafted Jevon, some of the things he did, athletically, were incredible," Titans coach Jeff Fisher said.

It didn't take Kearse long to show off, either. The Titans' first-round pick in 1999 (16th overall) gave his new team a taste on the very first day of his first camp, according to Fisher. "We were doing some testing, the vertical jump, with the bar with the swatches you hit. We were at the temporary facility in Bellevue (a West Nashville neighborhood)," Fisher said. "Jevon walked in, looked around and said, 'Hey, if I push the ceiling tiles up can I leave?' Jerry Gray (a Titans assistant coach from 1997-2000) was manning that station and

he says, 'Just get over here and jump, Rook.' And he says, 'No, no, if I jump up and push the ceiling tiles can I leave?' 'Yeah, yeah, you can leave.'

"They were like 12 feet high. And he just stands there and jumps, pushes the ceiling tile over, comes back down to the ground and walks out the door."

It was the first of many times Kearse would make jaws hit the floor and eyes bulge out of their heads in his first season. The 6'4", 255-pounder was a holy terror as a rookie, hunting down quarterbacks like a cheetah after an antelope. Before it was all said and done in 1999, Kearse had rung up an NFL rookie-record 14.5 sacks and had led the league with 10 forced fumbles. "I thought he'd be productive, and I expected him to make a lot of plays as a rookie, but not this many," Fisher said.

Kearse was named NFL Defensive Rookie of the Year by the Associated Press and was named to the first of three consecutive Pro Bowls. "I wanted to show all the teams that passed me up…that they missed out, and I think I did a pretty good job of starting that," Kearse said.

Kearse earned 49 of the 50 first-place votes for the Defensive Player of the Year award. Someone inexplicably voted for Washington Redskins cornerback Champ Bailey. More importantly, the young defensive end was a big reason the Titans had their most successful season ever, reaching Super Bowl XXXIV.

"The impact he had on our defense was a primary reason for our success," Fisher said. "We were scoring points and getting up and when you can rush the passer and protect the lead, you can win games, and that's what we did. He just chased and made plays all over the field. He was one of the better defensive players we've had here."

Kearse remembers well that the season almost ended well before the Super Bowl. He had done his level best to push the Titans past the Buffalo Bills in the wild-card game, recording two sacks, a forced fumble, and a safety. But when Bills kicker Steve Christie booted a 41-yard field goal with 16 seconds remaining to put his team in front 16–15, even The Freak thought this one was The Done.

"My agent at the time, Leigh Steinberg, told me he was coming to watch (Bills defensive end) Bruce Smith play, and he was like, 'Oh, and you, you.' I had a couple of sacks. I was like, 'I played well, but there ain't no way now.' I played a great game, it was a great first season, I made the Pro Bowl, but no way were we gonna pull this out.

"Then the play [Homerun Throwback] started, and I was like, 'Yes, yes, yes!' I can still see it in my head, see [Kevin] Dyson coming by the sideline. I jumped up in the air as high as I could. It was unbelievable."

Of course Dyson scored in what became known as the Music City Miracle, and off the Titans went on their merry way to the Super Bowl. It had been quite a rookie season for Kearse, who already wondered what he'd do for an encore. He needn't have worried. Kearse continued to put up double-digit sack numbers the next two seasons as well. He had 11.5 in 2000 and 10 more in 2001.

But a freak injury cost The Freak most of the 2002 season, and it was the beginning of the end of his time in Nashville. The injury occurred in the 2002 season opener against the Philadelphia Eagles, on just the second play from scrimmage. Kearse was chasing down Eagles running back Dorsey Levens when he leaped to avoid teammate Henry Ford. When Kearse landed, the fifth metatarsal bone in his left foot fractured. He underwent surgery within days, but his recovery took longer than originally expected. When he did return, 13 games later, he simply didn't have the same explosiveness. He ended up playing just four games that season and registered two sacks.

Jevon Kearse's amazing rookie season in 1999 was a major reason for the Titans' success. (Scott Halleran/Allsport/Getty Images)

After four seasons with Philadelphia, Jevon Kearse returned to the Titans for the 2008 season.
(Photo by Kirby Lee/NFL/Getty Images)

It was a tough time for Kearse. He never had experienced anything in his playing career like the misery of the 2002 season. He ended up having a second surgery less than a month after the season. "It wasn't fun," Kearse said. "It was pretty tough inside. Besides being aggravated I was feeling like it was a punishment for something I did.

"At first I was miserable and hating myself. I didn't want to communicate with my friends and family. Pretty much the only communication I wanted to have was with my teammates, because those are the guys I feel connected with."

Kearse rehabbed and got himself ready to go in 2003, and he looked like The Freak of old. He had 9.5 sacks through nine games before he was hindered by an ankle sprain. He didn't manage another sack the rest of the season.

When the Titans were faced with a decision on whether to place the franchise tag on him in February 2004, which would have allowed them to keep him one more season, Fisher decided it would be too costly and let him go. On the first day of free agency, the Eagles signed Kearse to a long-term deal, the richest for a defensive end in league history at $66 million for eight years.

He played four seasons in Philadelphia, but he never felt like he was used correctly. Kearse had 7.5 sacks in each of his first two seasons with the Eagles. He was off to a great start in 2006 with 3.5 sacks through two games, but he sprained multiple ligaments in his left knee during Philadelphia's overtime loss to the New York Giants in Week 2 and never returned to the field. In 2007 he was benched in favor Juqua Thomas, a player who had been Kearse's backup with the Titans from 2001-03.

Rather than pay Kearse the $6.46 million he would be owed in 2008, the Eagles released him on Feb. 28. Guess who signed him a week later?

"A cap situation didn't allow us to hold onto him, but as we speak he's back and I'm confident you'll see some of the old Jevon over the next couple of years," Fisher said. "He's excited to be back. He's comfortable. He knows the system, knows the people and wants to get back to doing what he did.

"He says he wasn't used in their system the way he hoped to have been used. He knows he'll come back and be the same player he was because he'll be in a different alignment in a different technique doing different things than he did in Philadelphia."

Kearse said he can't wait to be The Freak again. "That's what brought me back," the 10-year veteran said. "I feel like here they're going to put me in a position to make plays. I want to get back on the field and prove to the world that I still have it."

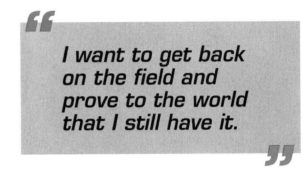

I want to get back on the field and prove to the world that I still have it.

DERRICK MASON

To hear Derrick Mason's voice is to get an immediate peek at his personality. He's high-pitched and high-strung. It's an almost perfect match.

Mason started his career with the Oilers/Titans after being taken in the fourth round (98th pick overall) of the 1997 NFL Draft. He was not an immediate hit. In fact, Mason struggled in his first three seasons with the team. He caught only 47 passes during the stretch from 1997-99. Coach Jeff Fisher wasn't sure Mason would stick. There was no indication that the player they had drafted would become one of the NFL's leading receivers over the next handful of seasons.

"There was a time early in Mase's career where he was on the bubble," Fisher said. "He was struggling with route concepts. He didn't get going till year three or four."

Yes, it was lucky No. 4. As in both the team and Mason were lucky he was still around.

"I think they showed a lot of patience staying with me, basically giving me time to catch on and figure out what was going on," Mason said. "I really thank them for that. It pretty much worked out for both parties."

The former Michigan State wide receiver who paved the way for so many Spartans receivers to follow him to stardom in the NFL began to get on the same page with quarterback Steve McNair in the 2000 season. They became one of the league's most lethal combinations, developing that sense that comes only with time and long hours on the practice field.

Derrick Mason was a force on offense and special teams for the Titans. Here he scored a touchdown against the New England Patriots in a playoff game on January 10, 2004. (Photo by Al Bello/Getty Images)

"Words can't explain how important Derrick was to this ball club, especially being a quarterback and he's a receiver," McNair said. "The connection we made and the chemistry we had together, it was amazing."

McNair would scramble and Mason would follow. Or Mason would sit down in a zone and his QB would find him. Mason's reception totals quickly went from so-so to staggering. He caught 63 passes in 2000 for a then career-high 895 yards (14.2 average) and five touchdowns.

The Titans also began using Mason all over the field in 2000, and he responded with a record-setting season. His 895 receiving yards, 662 punt return yards, 1,132 kickoff return yards, and 1 rushing yard resulted in an NFL single-season record of 2,690 combined net yards, which topped the old mark of 2,535 by San Diego's Lionel James in 1985. Mason was named to his first Pro Bowl.

It was only the beginning. From 2001-2005, Mason was one of the most prolific receivers in the NFL. He caught 343 passes during that span for 4,611 yards and 29 touchdowns, most of it from McNair. In 2003 he made his second Pro Bowl, this time as a receiver and not a return specialist. He hauled in 95 passes for 1,303 yards and eight touchdowns.

"I think it's just Mason being football savvy," McNair said. "When you have a smart guy like that that's able to go out there and make adjustments on the run and doing the little things right, then you have to look for that guy. Mason is a guy that's very competitive; He's very nifty whether he's inside or outside. That's what separates the good ones from the great ones ... knowing the game and knowing when to make the adjustments and communicating with the quarterback."

Mason had mutual admiration for McNair.

"When he came out in '95, not many people were taking a chance on a lot of quarterbacks that played at small schools, much less a black quarterback back when there were so many stereotypes about African-American quarterbacks," Mason said. "'Can they lead a team? Are they smart enough? Can he be that franchise guy?' He was that kind of guy. He would have been great if he'd played in the '50s and '60s. He played football the way it was supposed to be played."

Mason was a great fit for the way Fisher likes his offenses to operate. He wasn't a burner or a big-play guy. He could go over the middle, make the tough catch, and keep the chains moving. He had the reliability of a possession receiver with the wiggle to work for more yardage. "There was a time there where he was catching 90-100 balls for us," Fisher said. "He was a huge part of our offense."

Ultimately Mason became another salary-cap casualty from the great Titans teams of the early 2000s. In March 2005, he signed as a free agent with the rival Baltimore Ravens, for whom he continued to put up big numbers, including a career-high 103 receptions in 2007.

"I was very disappointed that we were unable to keep him," Fisher said. "I enjoyed having him and enjoyed watching him develop and mature. It was very rewarding for me.

"He was one of my favorite players during that period of time. He always played with emotion. He'd inevitably end up apologizing for his frustrations in not getting the ball or whatever, but it was a result of how competitive he was. He just wanted the football."

CRAIG HENTRICH

Eight-letter word. Starts with an H.

Clue: Future Hall of Fame punter.

Titans coach Jeff Fisher knows the answer, and he's not even the one who is the crossword enthusiast.

Answer: H-e-n-t-r-i-c-h.

Craig Hentrich has been the only punter the Tennessee Titans have had since moving to Nashville in 1998. He has missed only one game in the last 14 seasons. That came in September 2007, against the New Orleans Saints, when back pain forced him to the sideline.

The Titans acquired the former Notre Dame punter/placekicker as an unrestricted free agent and made him the league's first $1 million punter. He has been a model of consistency, averaging at least 41.4 yards per punt in all but one of his seasons in the blue and red of the Titans. His 47.2-yard gross average in 1998 is the team's single-season record. His best punt, a 78-yarder against the Pittsburgh Steelers on Jan. 2, 2000, ranks second. He has been to the Pro Bowl twice, in 1998 and 2003. Hentrich also is one of the best of all-time at keeping opponents pinned inside their own 20.

Hentrich has, for all intents and purposes, become a security blanket for Fisher. The coach is wistful when he thinks about all the ways Hentrich has helped his team win games that have gone unnoticed.

"Beyond what he does with his foot and punting the ball away, people don't realize and can't appreciate how effective he has been as a holder," Fisher said. "He saved so many games for us on errant snaps. He has been terrific at getting bad snaps down. Then there's the threat he posed as a passer in the fake game, and he kicked off for a couple of years. Then you've got the pooch game, and he handles the kick onsides.

"He's a great athlete as a punter. He quietly goes about his job."

Hentrich tested the free-agent waters after the 2002 season, but he signed a six-year contract to remain with the Titans on June 25, 2003.

"I was optimistic the whole time," Hentrich said. "I knew they wanted me back here and I wanted to be back. Coach Fisher is just a great coach to play for. I played under Coach (Mike) Holmgren for five years and that was just a totally different ball game. He's more of an authoritarian.... Playing on edge all the time was kind of tough. Here, you're just relaxed. You just play your game and that's when I play the best…when I'm relaxed."

Former Titans wide receiver Drew Bennett was among the happiest players when Hentrich was re-signed. The former UCLA quarterback had been forced to take over Hentrich's holding duties in his absence. "You know, you never really know the name of a holder until he messes up," Bennett said. "Craig does an amazing job."

Hentrich couldn't resist poking a little fun at his temporary replacement. "I think the happiest guy whenever I walked in this morning was Drew Bennett," Hentrich said. "He didn't have to hold anymore. He didn't like that a whole lot. Joe (Nedney, the Titans' placekicker from 2001-04) gave him a couple of divots in the eye. I just told him, 'Welcome to my world.'"

Hentrich has quite an array of hobbies, which isn't unusual for punters. They usually have time on their hands. Hentrich is one of the NFL's best golfers. *Golf Digest* ranked the best golfers among 200 current and former athletes in its June 2007 issue and it ranked him fifth, the best among current and former NFL players and the best among current athletes.

Hentrich also is an avid crossword and Sudoku enthusiast. He says Titans Hall of Fame offensive lineman Bruce Matthews got him hooked when he first joined the team. Fisher said Hentrich amuses himself year after year watching different players come through Baptist Sports Park, especially the younger ones. That's life when you have the job security Hentrich does.

"He should be a Hall of Fame punter. I'll have a difficult time if he's ever gone," Fisher said. "You will not replace him. We'll get somebody who'll do a good job punting the ball. But you won't replace him. That (signing Hentrich in 1998) was one of the better decisions we made."

Eight-letter word. Starts with an R.

Clue: Word that best describes the only punter Tennessee Titans fans have ever known.

Answer: R-e-l-i-a-b-l-e.

Reliability has been a hallmark of Craig Hentrich's career. Hentrich is shown punting against the Indianapolis Colts on a 2005 regular-season game. (Photo by Doug Pensinger/Getty Images)

BRAD HOPKINS

The Houston Oilers traded up from 19th to 13th overall in the 1993 NFL Draft to take offensive tackle Brad Hopkins out of the University of Illinois, where he was an All-American as a senior. It turned out to be a very wise move. Thirteen years later he retired from the Tennessee Titans having made two Pro Bowl appearances and 188 starts at left tackle.

Hopkins was a tremendous athlete who was deserving of high praise for how he protected the blind side of quarterbacks such as Warren Moon and Steve McNair and opened holes for running back Eddie George, among others. He was the only left tackle McNair had during his Titans tenure, all 11 seasons.

"I trusted him completely, and that peace of mind that he was protecting my blindside allowed me to be a better quarterback and find the open receivers," McNair said.

"There's no tougher position to play in the National Football League than left tackle," said Jeff Fisher, who arrived as an assistant with the Oilers a year after Hopkins was drafted and soon became the head coach for the rest of Hopkins' career. "The players that he played against over the years and the job he did in the one-on-one battles against some of the better pass-rushers in the league from the Bruce Smiths to the Mike McCrarys, he held his own out there.

"It's hard to say how successful Steve would have been if we didn't have Brad over there. We were able to do things because we knew Brad could do his job. He was so athletic he could have played tight end in this league."

Hopkins, whom the Titans listed at 6'3", and 295 pounds, cracked the starting lineup in his rookie season. The accomplishment not only was significant for him—he went on to make the NFL's All-Rookie Team—but it allowed him for that one season to play alongside two future Hall of Famers, guard Mike Munchak and center (that season, anyway) Bruce Matthews. Munchak retired following the 1993 season, but Hopkins and Matthews played alongside each other until Matthews hung it up in 2001.

For Hopkins' final nine seasons with the franchise, Munchak was his offensive line coach. First he was tutored by the best, then one became his teacher. "I owe every single thing that I have ever accomplished or I have ever done or I've ever tried to understand on this field to Mike because he to me was… it's almost like he's my brain," Hopkins said at his retirement news conference. "It's like, when you have the fear to go out and try to accomplish something that's so great, and when you have someone like that that's, one, been through it and, two, can teach you how to go through it, I mean, that's all you need.

> ❝
> **There's no tougher position to play in the National Football League than left tackle…. He held his own out there.**
> ❞

"These guys I played with and the guys that coached me, that's what it's all about. Getting up and going to work wasn't hard because I was surrounded by guys that wanted to hold it together. The fight is hard. The competition is hard. But when you know that the guys surrounding you, you just have an innate love for each other, it makes it easy, and that's why we play this game."

Brad Hopkins prepares to block against the Seattle Seahawks in a 2005 regular-season game.
(Photo by Paul Spinelli/Getty Images)

Eddie George's best seasons, from 1996-2001, came when Matthews moved to left guard alongside Hopkins. There was little doubt which way the Titans would send George. It didn't mean anybody could stop the train or get out of the way of the two guys laying the track.

"He got me 10,000 yards," George said. "Every one of my yards was behind Brad. He's a rarity. His athleticism and his confidence as a left tackle made him unique. With the things he was able to do, you didn't have to worry about that left side at all and that's tough to come by in this league. Brad had a stellar career and hopefully he can be in the Hall of Fame one day because he is that caliber of player. But more importantly, it's what he meant in the locker room—his character and charisma. He's a big kid. It was a great relationship he had with all of us."

The Titans released Hopkins after the 2005 season. He considered playing elsewhere, and he visited with the New York Jets, Tampa Bay Buccaneers, and Atlanta Falcons. Ultimately he decided it was best to always be remembered as a Titan. "I've actually shed tears in the weight room with young kids that were released. It wasn't something that they had a choice in doing," Hopkins said. "For me, I kind of always said that I would hope I could go out on my own terms because the other way would be really too painful. So to say that I'm able to walk away from this game being still in one piece, for the most part, to me it's a great deal."

Nothing made Fisher prouder than to see Hopkins, like Matthews and tight end Frank Wycheck before him, retire as a Titan and still have a little left in his tank. "You think about Bruce and Brad and Frank…it's rare in the National Football League to walk away on your own terms, to realize 'Enough is enough, I'm gonna walk away with my head up and retire and go,'" Fisher said. "Most of the time someone is telling you you're done and you don't get another opportunity.

"They took it as far as they could. They realized at that point for whatever reason—time, whether it was a health reason or an age reason—it was time to walk away, and I admire that. They should serve as great examples to younger players. When younger players come into the league all they think about is their first snap. The reality is their last snap is out there, and it's pretty close. Only they can push that last snap away and out there years and years away. I can't do it for them, only they can. That's what Frank, Brad, Bruce, Eddie, those guys knew by taking care of themselves and working during the off-season and during the season that they could push their last snaps so far out there. For that they got to enjoy the benefits of a long career. Guys will come in here and not do that and their last snap creeps up on them before they know it."

SAMARI ROLLE

The head coach's job is to watch everything that goes on during practice and in games. But anyone who doesn't believe Jeff Fisher has a little extra focus on defensive backs is kidding themselves. He played defensive back at the University of Southern California, and his first job as an NFL coach was as an assistant in charge of defensive backs.

So when he tells you he watched Samari Rolle develop into a shutdown corner, you can believe the coach of the Tennessee Titans means the young charge has become a special player in the NFL.

Rolle was a second-round pick by the Titans in the 1998 draft. But it didn't take the former Florida State star long to become a fixture in the secondary. He saw action in 15 games as a rookie despite a scary injury during his first training camp, a concussion to his spinal cord that sidelined him for the final three preseason games and the regular-season opener.

"Samari came in and he battled. He overcame a difficult injury his rookie year on the practice field at TSU (Tennessee State University, where the Titans practiced temporarily until their practice facility was built)," Fisher said. "He earned the job quickly.

*Samari Rolle of the Tennessee Titans at training camp in 2004 in Nashville.
(Photo by Ronald C. Modra/Sports Imagery/Getty Images)*

"I think he just played for the first couple of years. During the off-season it was more important for him to go to South Beach than it was to come back here. So for two off-seasons we were trying to explain to him, 'You're better off here.' By the third off-season he said, 'I don't know what I was thinking, why I wasn't here.'"

Rolle led the Titans in interceptions from 1999-2001 and again in 2003. His finest season came in 2000. He tied for the AFC lead with seven interceptions, one of which he memorably returned 81 yards for a touchdown on a Monday night. The Titans were in Washington to play the Redskins on Oct. 20, 2000. Tennessee led 13–7 with just 10 seconds before halftime, but the Redskins had the ball at the Titans' 34 and were looking to cut into the lead, if not erase it altogether. Quarterback Brad Johnson dropped to pass and looked in the direction of wide receiver Irving Fryar.

Rolle stepped in front and made the interception then began downfield, weaving his way through seemingly every Redskins offensive player. Time had expired, so it was end zone or bust as the Titans corner crisscrossed the field and no doubt covered a lot more than the 81 yards for which he received credit. By the time he reached the end zone, Rolle was so exhausted he required an injury timeout to catch his breath.

"Two football fields, nonstop," Rolle said. "Luckily, I saw nobody was around me and that was when the rest of the blockers came."

In addition to being a shut-down corner, Samari Rolle proved himself to be an effective run-stopper for the Titans. (Photo by Craig Jones/Getty Images)

"It was a huge play," Fisher said. "Everybody knew the time was out and it was either you get in the end zone or you don't."

The Titans went on to win 27–21, thanks in large part to Rolle's big play. It was the sixth-longest interception return in franchise history.

As the years went by, Rolle relied less on his athleticism and more on his study habits. The combination made him one of the best corners in the game during his years in the blue and red. "When he dedicated himself to the game and the off-season and eliminated some distractions in his life, he became a really, really talented player," Fisher said. "Samari understood this: As a defensive back when you plant and drive and you make an interception, that's a really good play based on your ability. Better than that is the play you make because you recognize the formation, motion, set, or a split, and you anticipated a route that you studied all week and you guessed right and made the play. That's more fulfilling than just making a play based on athletic ability.

"By his third year that was the player Samari was. You couldn't outsmart Samari because he became such a quiet student at the cornerback position. He's doing it to this day. Watching some of these younger players mature and realize some of those things on their own was very gratifying. Samari would pick off passes in practice on a daily basis because he knew what we were going to do. He became a really good player, a true shutdown corner."

Shutdown corners don't come cheap in the NFL. The Titans released Rolle after the 2004 season because of salary-cap reasons. He signed as an unrestricted free agent with the Baltimore Ravens, for whom he has played since.

On Nov. 21, 2007, he revealed that he had been diagnosed with epilepsy, a common chronic neurological disorder that is characterized by recurrent unprovoked seizures. It had an obvious effect on him during the season, but he vowed to continue playing because medicine was keeping his seizures under control.

"I thought at first I would never be able to play (again)," Rolle said at a news conference that day in Baltimore. "In my locker today, I walked in and (read) that (Pittsburgh's) Alan Faneca has had epilepsy since he was 15. He's probably the best guard in football. So, I feel very good. Knowing what I know now and with the way last year was for me, I'm not ending my career like that. That's what I'm most proud of."

SUPER SEASON

by Jim Wyatt

In 1999, they went from Oilers to Titans.

And after three straight 8–8 seasons when they didn't have a place to call home, they moved into a brand new stadium across the Cumberland River from downtown Nashville. It was an inaugural season that turned out to be an unforgettable one as well. And from the first preseason game, it didn't take long for everyone to realize it was the start of something special.

YEAH, IT WAS THE PRESEASON, BUT...

In the Houston Oilers' last game at the Astrodome in 1996, only 15,131 fans turned out. A year later, as Tennessee Oilers, they played in front of sparse crowds at the Liberty Bowl in Memphis, followed by a season when support was lukewarm at Vanderbilt Stadium. Finally, on August 27, 1999, they had a new name—Tennessee Titans—and a place they could call home and feel appreciated.

Tennessee Titans quarterback Steve McNair escapes the shoestring tackle of St. Louis Rams defensive end Kevin Carter (93) during Super Bowl XXXIV. McNair's scramble kept the Titans' final drive of the game alive. (Photo by Al Pereira/NFL/Getty Images)

Sure, it was only a preseason game, but it was clear to everyone on hand at the first-ever game at the Coliseum it was much more. Country music artist Faith Hill was there to sing the national anthem. NFL Commissioner Paul Tagliabue was also in the house. Boxing announcer Michael Buffer announced the lineups for the game against the Atlanta Falcons, televised by ESPN. And T-Rac made his official debut as the team's mascot.

"We're at home now, finally after four years," owner Bud Adams said. "What else could you ask for? It's exhilarating, just exhilarating…. It's everything I imagined it would be."

On the historic night, a preseason crowd of 65,729 qualified as the largest home crowd in the history of the franchise. The Titans ended up winning, 17–3. On their first play from scrimmage, quarterback Neil O'Donnell, playing for the injured Steve McNair, connected with receiver Yancey Thigpen for a 48-yard completion. Falcons running back Jamal Anderson was among those who left impressed.

"Tennessee, Houston, whatever," Anderson said. "That was a heck of an atmosphere. That was great for football and it's going to be great for that team."

The Titans ended up winning all eight regular-season home games in '99, as well as their only home playoff game.

A GREAT START

After all the hype leading up to the season, the Titans faced an old rival in the first regular-season game at the Coliseum. And at the start, the Cincinnati Bengals looked like they'd be easy prey.

But what unfolded on Sept. 12, 1999 set the stage for what turned out to be a magical season. It was the first of many nail-biters and a game when quarterback Steve McNair began to make a name for himself in Nashville, despite resistance from some fans who needed to be further convinced along the way.

The Titans jumped out to a 26–7 lead in the first half, and the stadium rocked. Things quickly unraveled after that, though, as the Bengals scored 28 unanswered points to take a 35–26 lead early in the fourth quarter. It looked like past days all over again. That's when a hobbling McNair, booed by some when he came jogging back onto the field with 7:56 remaining, led the charge back and turned out to be a hero. McNair had fumbled the previous possession.

McNair drove the Titans 70 yards on 9 plays, finishing with a swing pass to running back Eddie George that turned into a 17-yard touchdown with 4:30 to play. McNair's third touchdown pass of the game cut Cincinnati's lead to 35–33. The Titans' defense then held the Bengals to a three-and-out, setting the stage for the final rally.

The Titans took over at the Bengals' 49 with 2:24 remaining. McNair completed passes to George, tight end Frank Wycheck, and receiver Yancey Thigpen on the final drive, moving the ball to the Cincinnati 15-yard line with just 12 seconds left. On came kicker Al Del Greco, who booted the game-winning field goal from 33 yards out to give the Titans a 36–35 win. A team that endured so much misfortune in recent years suddenly appeared on a different path.

"The way we won, I hope it's indicative of the new approach of this team," veteran offensive lineman Bruce Matthews said. "We found a way to win, even though it was as bleak as it's been at any time in the past. It's the type of win that determines whether we keep playing in January or not."

T-Rac, the mascot of the Tennessee Titans, debuted in 1999. (Photo by Kevin C. Cox/Getty Images)

For McNair, it took a little longer for him to answer all of his critics. But his performance—he completed 21-of-32 passes for 341 yards and three touchdowns—was a start.

"He had a career-game—period," George said. "He did a great job throwing the ball. He handled the adversity well."

TITANIC SHOWDOWN

In time, it would be known as Super Bowl XXXIV½, though no one knew it when the Titans squared off against the previously unbeaten St. Louis Rams on Halloween.

Yes, before Super Bowl XXXIV, the two teams played in the regular season. And what happened without question got the nation's attention.

The Rams not only entered the game unbeaten at 6–0, they looked untouchable. Quarterback Kurt Warner had already thrown 18 touchdown passes in the first six games, and the Rams had outscored their opponents by just under 26 points per game.

The Titans were 5–1—their only loss to San Francisco in Week 4—and they got an extra emotional boost by the return of quarterback Steve McNair, who had missed the previous five games after back surgery.

Before the biggest—and loudest—crowd to date at the Coliseum, the Titans jumped out to a 21–0 lead in the first quarter as McNair threw two touchdown passes and ran for another. But the Rams fought back, outscoring the Titans 21–3 to make it 24–21 with 2:14 left. The Rams had a chance to tie the game in the closing seconds but missed a 38-yard field goal, and the Titans held on for the win. It set off a wild celebration on the field, as the Titans improved to 6–1.

"This was a statement game sent around the country," Titans fullback Lorenzo Neal said. "Everybody was talking about the Rams. Hey, the Titans are for real."

McNair was a question mark leading up to kickoff because of his back, but he ended up completing 13 of 29 passes for 186 yards and two touchdowns in the game. The Rams ended up out-gaining the Titans in yardage, 415–281, but the Titans sacked Warner six times and found a way to win.

"We had a tough time," Rams coach Dick Vermeil said. "We haven't been in this kind of atmosphere. We haven't been under this kind of pressure before."

FREAKED OUT

Rams offensive tackle Fred Miller got spooked on Halloween—by Titans rookie defensive end Jevon Kearse. Miller committed six false starts and a holding penalty while facing Kearse, who finished with five tackles, a sack, two quarterback pressures, and a forced fumble in Tennessee's 24–21 win. It was one of 15 penalties for the Rams in the game.

"He might be jumping in his sleep," Kearse joked after the game. "His eyes were so big, just watching me.... After a while, I just started looking at him and laughing at him, trying to get in his head."

Eventually, the two players became teammates and friends with the Titans, as Miller signed as an unrestricted free agent prior to the 2000 season. And they were able to laugh about the events of that Sunday afternoon in October. Miller ended up doing a solid job against Kearse when the two teams squared off again in the Super Bowl, but he was admittedly humiliated by Kearse in the October meeting in Nashville.

The Titans met the St. Louis Rams during the 1999 regular season, prior to their showdown in the Super Bowl. In the Halloween game, Tennessee earned a 24–21 win. (Jonathan Daniel/Allsport/Getty Images)

"I needed a couple of days to get through it," Miller said. "I went home and really just sat down with my family, looked at my son and saw how he loved me and my wife.... My dogs treated me great."

REASON TO CELEBRATE

The Titans had won some big games leading up to a Week 15 contest against the Falcons, but after their 30–17 win over Atlanta at the Coliseum on Dec. 19, 1999, there was clearly reason to celebrate. It clinched the team's first playoff berth in Tennessee and the franchise's first playoff berth since the 1993 season.

After heading into the locker room after the game, the Titans returned to the field and celebrated with their fans. Players took a victory lap around the stadium, slapping high-fives with those in the front row. It was a curtain call that nearly brought some to tears.

"This is especially good for all the guys who have been through the last four years," said kicker Al Del Greco, referring to the team's travels from Houston to Memphis to Nashville. "Jevon Kearse and the new guys appreciate it, too. But it has a deeper meaning for a lot of us."

The Titans won it by forcing six turnovers on defense. Quarterback Steve McNair threw for 216 yards and ran for 76 more. "The playoffs were our first goal," receiver Isaac Byrd said. "But we've got a lot more goals to accomplish."

MUSIC CITY MIRACLE

The play was called "Homerun Throwback."

It really had no business working. It probably wouldn't work in the backyard 9 out of 10 times, let alone in an NFL game, a playoff game no less. But it worked when the Titans played the Buffalo Bills on Jan. 8, 2000, in an AFC Wild Card Playoff Game at Adelphia Coliseum.

No Titans coach, player, or fan will ever forget the moment. The "Music City Miracle" already has become a part of NFL lore, ranking with the "Immaculate Reception" among the greatest finishes in playoff history.

Of course, you can't stage a miracle unless your team is losing. The Titans entered the game as the favorites. They had gone 13–3 during the regular season and had handed AFC Central rival and top seed Jacksonville its only two losses. Tennessee also was playing at home, where coach Jeff Fisher's team hadn't lost during the 1999 season. The Bills, meanwhile, were 11–5 and runner-up to the Indianapolis Colts in the AFC East.

Going into the game, the Bills had opted to start Rob Johnson at quarterback instead of Doug Flutie. It was a surprising move in light of the fact that Flutie had started the first 15 games of the season and had put Buffalo in position to be in the playoffs. With Flutie sitting out the final regular-season game against the Colts because the Bills had clinched a playoff spot, Johnson came in and led them to a 31–6 triumph. It was an impressive offensive showing, but the Colts had rested many of their starters. Indianapolis couldn't improve its playoff position either. It was going to enter the AFC playoffs as the No. 2 seed, behind the Jaguars.

There was much debate that week in Buffalo about who should start at quarterback. The speculation was coach Wade Phillips wanted to go with Flutie but that he was overruled by the front office. The game between the Bills and Titans was scoreless after the first quarter, and the play hardly had been crisp. Johnson was sacked the first time he dropped back to pass, when Josh Evans broke through and took him down. The Titans couldn't muster any offense in the first quarter, either.

Tennessee opened the scoring in the second quarter when defensive end Jevon Kearse chased down Johnson in the end zone for a safety. The Titans quickly made it 9–0 after Derrick Mason returned the ensuing free kick 42 yards to the Bills' 28. They needed five plays to cover the distance, with quarterback Steve McNair going the final yard for the touchdown on a bootleg around the right end.

After forcing a punt, the Titans drove 56 yards in 11 plays to get in position for kicker Al Del Greco. He missed from 45 yards, but the Bills were called for holding. The five-yard penalty gave Del Greco another shot, and he was good from 40 on the final play of the half to push the Titans' lead to 12–0.

Tennessee's defense had stymied Johnson and the Bills. They had managed only 64 yards of total offense in the first 30 minutes, and the Titans had sacked Johnson three times. Kearse was a holy terror against the makeshift Buffalo offensive line. But the Bills rallied, and they started on the first play from scrimmage in the third quarter when Antowain Smith burst through for a 44-yard run. Four plays later, Smith scored from four yards out to cut the lead to 12–7. The drive covered 62 yards, nearly all of Buffalo's first-half total.

The Titans now were the team struggling offensively. Bills defensive end Bruce Smith was getting pressure on McNair, and Buffalo was keeping Titans running back Eddie George in check. The third quarter ended with the score still 12–7.

Jevon Kearse tries to get past an Atlanta Falcons lineman during a December 19, 1999 game. (Photo by David Drapkin/Getty Images)

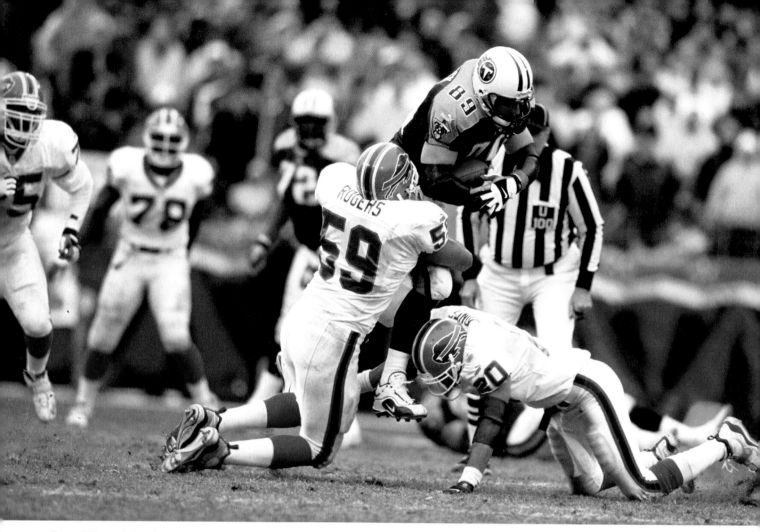

Frank Wycheck battles for extra yardage in the Titans' AFC Wildcard Playoff Game on January 8, 2000. The game would be eventually decided by the Music City Miracle. (Photo by Allen Kee/NFL/Getty Images)

The Bills had the ball when the final 15 minutes started, and they maneuvered down the field for the go-ahead score with 11:08 to play. The drive covered 65 yards, 52 of it coming on a 37-yard pass from Johnson to Eric Moulds coupled with a roughing-the-passer penalty on Kearse. Smith finished the drive with another four-yard touchdown run, and the Bills led 13–12. They went for the two-point conversion, but Johnson's pass to receiver Kevin Williams was incomplete.

The teams traded punts before the Titans got the ball back. Isaac Byrd's 16-yard punt return set Tennessee up at the Buffalo 36. Five consecutive carries by George netted 17 tough yards, and Del Greco managed to hit a 36-yard field goal to put the Titans back in front, 15–13, with just 1:48 to play.

On the ensuing drive, with no timeouts remaining, Johnson led the Bills on a five-play, 37-yard drive to the Titans' 24. The quarterback played without a shoe for the final two plays, having lost one while scrambling and not having time to put it back on with the clock running. With only 16 seconds remaining, Bills kicker Steve Christie nailed a 41-yard field goal to put Buffalo in the lead, 16–15.

The Bills believed they had put an end to a three-game playoff losing streak. Defensive back Daryl Porter was seen on the sidelines screaming, "This is our house! Our house, baby!" Bruce Smith, who had been superb in recording 2½ sacks, had on a blue Bills cap and was smiling and chirping, "To be a champion, you gotta win on the road, baby. Gotta win on the road."

Porter and Smith apparently had forgotten about the 16 seconds that remained. They were about to fall down on their heads like 16 tons.

Trailing by a point and about to receive Christie's kickoff, Titans head coach Jeff Fisher and special teams coach Allan Lowry called for "Homerun Throwback." Believe it or not, the Titans had practiced the play once a week during the regular season, every Saturday during special-teams walkthroughs.

"This was the first year we practiced the play. It was new," Fisher said. "Prior to that, Stanford-Cal was the play.... Alan came to me that offseason and said let's change it to this, and I said sure. And we designed it and put it in."

If the devil is in the details, Fisher is Satan himself. He always has prepared his team for every possible situation. If there is a stone unturned, the NFL's longest-tenured coach will find a backhoe. The players didn't always appreciate the method to his madness when practices were running long because he was going over "what-if" scenarios, but they never understood it better than when they pulled off the miracle.

"Another one of Jeff Fisher's crazy setups," veteran Titans safety Blaine Bishop said. "You name the situation. Ten seconds to go, we take an intentional safety. Just before halftime, we call a fair catch and try a free kick. Whatever it is, we'll practice it. Guys will be tired and rolling their eyes like, 'Yeah, this will ever come up.'"

The Titans had never used Homerun Throwback in a game situation. Let's face it, you really can't use it more than once. But this was as good a time as any. The play called for whoever received the ball to get it to Frank Wycheck, who was lined as the second man on the right in an alignment that had five players up front, four in the middle, and two deep men. The right-handed tight end then was to take a couple of steps forward as though he would return the ball, turn, and throw a lateral all the way across the field to a waiting Derrick Mason, one of the deep men. If it worked correctly, Mason would make the catch and have a wall of blockers.

Only Mason wasn't available.

"When Christie kicked the field goal, Alan and I simultaneously said 'Homerun Throwback,'" Fisher said. "So I'm looking for Mase, and the trainer says Mase is out with a concussion. So I started looking for Anthony Dorsett. He had practiced the play, too, as Mase's backup. But he was cramping up. So it was go find Dice (wide receiver Kevin Dyson).

"Hey, Kev, we're gonna run 'Homerun Throwback.' He says, literally, 'Coach, I really never paid attention.' So it was, 'Look, we think Isaac (Byrd) is gonna get the ball. He may kick it deep. If he doesn't I want you to stay outside the numbers over here by our bench and stay five yards behind the ball and wait, because you're our last outlet.' He says, 'I got you, coach.'"

> **Another one of Jeff Fisher's crazy setups. Whatever it is, we'll practice it. Guys will be tired and rolling their eyes like, 'Yeah, this will ever come up.'**

Dyson admits he got caught up in a whirlwind of events. He had been on the sidelines during the Bills' field-goal drive discussing what the Titans would do in a two-minute drill type of situation with McNair, Eddie George, Yancey Thigpen, and the offensive coaching staff. Suddenly he was being called on for the kick-return team, and he had no idea why.

"They were saying, 'You're gonna replace Mason and Dorsett,' and the nerves took over," Dyson said. "I was not completely sure of my responsibility. Byrd explained it to me and Alan is screaming at me as I'm going on the field, then Frank said something. Next thing you know I'm lining up.

"I'd seen them work on it each Saturday. But they worked different scenarios. I wasn't too confident. I was like, 'What do I do if it's kicked to me? Do I run, do I pitch to somebody else?' I knew the gist of the play, but it didn't work out like what I had seen."

That was mostly because the Bills didn't attempt a bounding, squib kick. They elected to try a pooch kick, a short, high ball designed to give their defenders time to race down field and limit any kind of return. Of all of the things Fisher had anticipated, this was not one of them.

"We worked deep kicks, practiced squib kicks that would go to a couple of different players," Fisher said. "We never worked a high pooch kick before. When the ball went up in the air I had some reservations. My initial thinking was, 'Well, Lo (Lorenzo Neal), could fair catch this.' We just needed a field goal. We had some time, could have made a play or two, kicked a field goal. Lo had the presence of mind to get the ball to Frank, particularly because he didn't want anything to do with the football. It was kind of, 'Here, you take it.'"

> **Hey, Kev, we're gonna run 'Homerun Throwback.' He says, literally, 'Coach, I really never paid attention.'**

Neal, who also was in the middle line, fielded the ball cleanly. Wycheck had drifted over next to Neal, and Neal made a handoff to Wycheck as he continued toward the right sideline. Wycheck then stopped and in one motion turned and threw a jump pass toward the opposite sideline.

Had the Bills kicked deep, the other deep man, Byrd, would have been the one to start right and then throw back across the field to Dyson. But the Titans were hoping for Wycheck to be the one with the ball in his hands. Earlier in the season he had thrown a 61-yard touchdown pass to Byrd, and the coaches were confident he could deliver the pass in this crucial situation.

"The conversation with me, Lorenzo and Jackie Harris, my wings, they were next to me, was, 'No way I'm throwing this,'" Wycheck said. "They said, 'Come get it, we're getting it to you.'

"It was strange. I knew I had to take some steps to sell it. It was weird. Everything felt like slow motion. They had a linebacker, No. 59, Rogers, I remember him almost stopping, not darting at me and trying to take a shot. He almost was confused and stopped. I have a photo of it and he's just kind of standing there.

"I didn't see where I was throwing. I just knew I had to throw it backward. I threw across my body, but it went backward. It kind of looked forward."

Certainly to all of Buffalo it looked forward. Wycheck threw a decent-enough spiral from the 25-yard line toward Dyson, who was all the way on the left end. He also was fairly alone. He was straddling the 25 as he caught the ball down around his ankles. He looked up and saw a handful of blockers and precious few Bills.

Wycheck didn't know at the time that Mason was out of the game.

"Isaac Byrd was gonna be the guy I was gonna throw it to," Wycheck said. "But the kick was high and short, he tripped up and fell down, and Dyson was the trail guy. He made himself available. I didn't even realize it was Dyson at the time. I was just worried about my own deal, I was so stressed about it."

Despite the pooch kick, Fisher saw the play unfolding nicely.

"I was downfield a little bit," Fisher said. "I saw Kevin get the ball and start running and I was thinking, 'Kevin, get what you can and get out of bounds, get out of bounds! And we'll kick the field goal.' Then I saw the wall and just said, 'Go, go! This is gonna happen.'"

Dyson raced 75 yards with what might as well have been a police escort. No one from Buffalo was even in the vicinity of stopping him. Christie was the only Bill with even a remote chance, and he was wiped out of the play by linebacker Terry Killens.

The Coliseum record crowd of 66,782 was in a state of delirium. Fisher and quarterback Steve McNair hugged. Dyson was mobbed in the end zone. Wycheck fell face first to the turf, where defensive lineman Dan Salave'a was the first to greet him with a hug when he rolled over, and safety Marcus Robertson piled on them. As Wycheck came off the field, he blew a kiss with both hands to the crowd.

The Bills were in a state of shock and disbelief. Their best hope was that the play would be overturned by the officials, who had been notified from the booth that they should review the play. Had it been a forward lateral? You'd be hard-pressed to call any of the angles referee Phil Luckett had to look at conclusive. Wycheck's right arm was just in front of the 25 as he jumped, twisted, and let go of the ball. Dyson, who had stopped and turned to face across the field, caught the ball straddling the 26, with his right cleat on the 25. He stooped low and caught it just above that shoe.

> **Think about what you just saw. It certainly makes you sit back and say, 'Maybe there is such a thing as fate.' If there is, why not us? Why not now?**
>
> **—General Manager Floyd Reese**

"I didn't have to catch the ball because it was a lateral, but in my mind I'm thinking, 'I have to catch this, it will be a smoother transition.' Once I caught [it] I looked up and started running. I was thinking, 'Get out of bounds! Get out of bounds!' But there was nobody there.

"I never had doubt it was a legit play. I didn't realize it was that close until I saw the replay. I didn't understand the review. I thought I was so far back. You don't realize in the game how close it was, you're in the moment. When I got home I was like, 'That's what the fuss was about.' It's legit, I made sure I was back. I took a good hard step back trying to get behind him. But the ball was right down the line of scrimmage."

The Bills weren't going to take Dyson's word. The minutes Luckett spent under the tarp looking at the play on the sidelines seemed like hours to Bills coach Phillips and his team. Phillips appeared preternaturally calm on the sidelines. ABC/ESPN announcers Mike Patrick, Joe Theismann, and Paul Maguire speculated that he was confident the play would be overturned and called a forward pass. At first Patrick and Maguire concurred, but as Dyson's return was replayed over and over, Theismann interjected that it was too close to call. As the three men in the booth tossed it around, they became convinced the play was a lateral.

"You know where it looks like a lateral more than any other time? Watch when he throws the ball back," Maguire said. "He throws it behind him. He's not throwing it forward. If you look at Wycheck's arm and body motion, he is throwing the ball back."

The replay took 1 minute, 59 seconds, according to ABC's time clock. Turns out all it did was give Titans fans another chance to celebrate.

"After reviewing the play on the field," Luckett announced, "it was a lateral."

The Bills were apoplectic. The home crowd crossed from excitement into utter delirium. Fisher could hardly hear himself think.

"The first thing I saw during the play when Frank threw it, I saw (line judge) Byron Boston go like this [motions], meaning it's a lateral," Fisher said. "Byron ran up and got in position and he pointed backward. So the next thing going through my mind is I don't think they can overturn it because it's too close. But if they do, what are we gonna do? How much time will they put back on the clock, we're gonna be penalized, and then we need to make a play.

"The next thing in my mind is if it is good, I gotta go for two. Because that put us up by five. The process was as we were waiting and waiting and waiting, I didn't think we could execute an offensive play after all that euphoria. And so I kicked the extra point."

> **That was the most dramatic finish I've seen in 40 years of football. I have never seen anything like that. It probably won't be seen again either.**
>
> **—Owner Bud Adams**

Al Del Greco's kick made the score 22–16 with 3 seconds to play. The Titans hadn't won a playoff game since 1991, but they were on the verge. Fisher's decision to kick the extra point almost came back to haunt him. The Bills used the Stanford-Cal play on the ensuing kickoff and reached midfield before the Titans stopped them. The clock read 0:00. The "Music City Miracle" was in the books. Titans 22, Bills 16.

The Bills said they were jobbed. From owner Ralph Wilson on down they believed they'd been cheated. "They felt like they were going to win the game, and then they thought it was taken away from them," Phillips said.

"The whole game, they gave them calls," Bills linebacker Gabe Northern said. "I don't know, maybe I am not supposed to speak on it, but the whole game we came out and we played hard and we fought and we earned a victory. But through different ways, it was taken away from us.

"What's going to happen, especially on the last call, they'll send it in (to the league) and show that it was a forward pass, then they will call us back and say, 'You were right.' But we will still be at home."

At home later that night with assistant coaches, family, and friends, Fisher admired his handiwork as "Homerun Throwback" was dissected as though it were the Zapruder film.

"You start to hear all of the stories about who saw it and who didn't, who left and who didn't, who went to the restroom," Fisher said. "Back at my house we had a bunch of people over—coaches, friends. It's getting played over and over again.

> "Now I see why we work on that play on Saturdays. Some of us thought it was a waste of time. Now I'm glad we work on it.
>
> —Running back Eddie George

"On the play, as you look at the screen and Kevin Dyson is running down the sideline, down on the edge of the white about the 5-yard line is this little kid going like this [Fisher makes a windmill motion with his right arm]. That was my 14-year-old son. He was handling the Polaroids on the sideline. He says, 'Dad I made TV, I made TV!' I said, 'Do you know what would have happened if you had bumped that official in the white? None of this would have happened. It wouldn't have counted.' He got real quiet. And I said, 'Naw, I'm just kidding. It would have been enforced on the kickoff.'"

The play affected the fortunes of both franchises. The Titans immediately turned it into gold, making a run to the Super Bowl. The Bills subsequently fired special teams coach Bruce DeHaven, who had been with the franchise for 13 years, a mere two days later. Phillips was fired a year later and replaced by Titans defensive coordinator Gregg Williams. Buffalo hasn't been in the playoffs since.

"You still hear stories from people who were listening on the radio at intersections and the light turned green and nobody moved," Fisher said. "And then when it was good, everybody was celebrating in the intersections."

Wycheck said he never pops in the tape to relive the moment, but he doesn't mind that it comes up every year for wild-card weekend.

"The longer I'm out of the game the more special it is in a way," said Wycheck, who retired after the 2003 season. "I get to almost relive it every year. I said after it happened that I couldn't realize the impact right then and there. As my kids get older, when my grandkids can see it.... It's kind of weird the Lord picked me to be in that situation. But I'm thankful. It brings back great memories."

Memories no one associated with the Titans will ever forget. Dyson has had an interesting association with the Miracle. Time has helped him put it in a much better perspective.

"For me when I was going through it, I didn't want to talk about it because I didn't want it to be my legacy," Dyson said. "I figured it was something I could look back on when I retired. But I didn't have the storybook career. I had a lot of injuries. I didn't have the 800 career catches, the perennial Pro Bowls, the three Super Bowl rings.

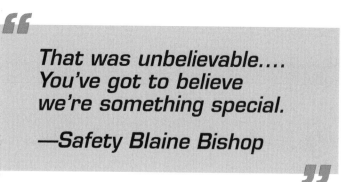

> *That was unbelievable....*
> *You've got to believe*
> *we're something special.*
>
> **—Safety Blaine Bishop**

"But I did have something left. I'm not a forgotten name, and lots of guys are. For every Jerry Rice there are 10 Kevin Dysons. But every year for the next however many years, people will say I remember that play, I remember you, I remember that name."

There are worse things to be remembered for than your role in a miracle.

ON THE AIR

The radio call of the "Music City Miracle" by Mike Keith and Pat Ryan on the Tennessee Titans Radio Network instantly became legendary across the network's listening area. This is the transcript of the call.

Keith: Do the Titans have a miracle left in them in what has been a magical season to this point? If they do, they need it now. Christie kicks it high and short. Gonna be fielded by Lorenzo Neal at the 25; he dishes it back to Wycheck; he throws it across the field to Dyson...

Ryan: He's got somethin'...

Keith: 30, 40...

Ryan: He's got somethin'...

Keith: 50, 40...

Ryan: He's got it! He's got it!

Keith (voice volume increasing): 30, 20...

Ryan: He's got it!

Keith: 10, 5, end zone...touchdown, Titans! There are no flags on the field! It's a miracle! Tennessee has pulled a miracle! A miracle for the Titans!

Then came the two-plus minute delay while the officials reviewed the play. When referee Phil Luckett returned to the playing field, Keith picked up his call.

Keith: Here comes Luckett, with the call of the new millennium.

When he announced his ruling, Keith and Ryan had another historic exchange.

Luckett: After reviewing the play, the ruling on the field stands. It was a lateral.

Keith: We did it!

Ryan: Yes! Titans win!

Keith: Three seconds to go, and Tennessee is on the verge of a miracle finish!

THE MAN BEHIND THE MIRACLE

While an assistant coach with the Dallas Cowboys in 1982, Titans special teams coach Alan Lowry saw Southern Methodist beat Texas Tech 34–27 when return man Bobby Leach took a cross-field lateral on a kickoff and raced 91 yards for a touchdown.

The play stuck in his head, and nearly 20 years later, he put it to use with the Music City Miracle, the improbable play the Titans used to beat the Buffalo Bills on January, 8, 2000, in the playoffs.

When Lowry was moved from wide receivers coach to special teams coach prior to the '99 season, he put "Homerun Throwback" in the team's playbook. "I had seen it work one time, so you always hope it will work again like that, but there are no guarantees with a play like that," Lowry said.

It worked, of course. Trailing 16–15 in the final moments, fullback Lorenzo Neal fielded a kickoff from Bills kicker Steve Christie, turned around, and gave it to tight end Frank Wycheck. He then threw a cross-field lateral to receiver Kevin Dyson, who raced 75 yards for a touchdown to give the Titans a 22–16 win over the Bills.

"It's a one-shot deal and it happened to work," Lowry said.

In the locker room after the game, many of the Titans admitted they hardly even paid attention when the play was practiced, some weeks in a hotel ballroom the day before a game. Also, many of the players who were supposed to be involved in the play—Dyson was the third option behind Derrick Mason and Anthony Dorsett—were injured and unavailable.

"What you have to sell them on is that when we're in a situation like that you have to have a play, and this is our play and we have to execute and make it work," Lowry said. "Now we just have to come up with another one."

CLOSE GAMES

Seven of Tennessee's games in 1999 were decided by three points or less, and each of the seven were decided in the final two minutes. The Titans fared well in those games, compiling a 6–1 mark in games decided by three points or less.

RACING BY INDY

Colts quarterback Peyton Manning probably never figured he'd be forced to use a silent count in a home playoff game. But that's exactly what happened at the RCA Dome in Indianapolis on Jan 16, 2000, the day the Titans silenced the Indianapolis Colts in a 19–16 win in the AFC Divisional Playoff Game.

And that's because a good number of the 57,097 fans on hand were from Nashville, cheering for the Titans. What they witnessed was the Titans advancing to their first AFC Championship Game since 1979. The Titans did it thanks to the longest touchdown run of running back Eddie George's career, a stifling defense, and some good eyes from a few folks on the sideline.

Trailing 9–6, George broke free on a 68-yard touchdown run to give Tennessee a 13–9 lead. He completed the memorable run looking up at the RCA video board ahead of him, making sure no one was closing in for a last-second tackle. It was part of a 162-yard day for George.

On defense, the Titans harassed Manning throughout the game, keeping him off rhythm and forcing him into one incompletion after another.

The biggest emotional swing in the game came with the Titans leading 16–9. Colts return man Terrence Wilkins fielded a punt and returned it 87 yards to the Titans' 3 in the fourth quarter. Suddenly, Indianapolis looked poised to tie the game at 16-all. And Colts fans were beginning to get loud.

SACK ATTACK

After registering just 30 sacks for the entire 1998 season, the Titans set a new franchise record by piling up 54 sacks in 1999, eclipsing the old mark of 52 set back in 1992. It was the third-best total in the NFL in '99, behind only Jacksonville (57) and St. Louis (54). Defensive end Jevon Kearse led the way with 14.5 sacks.

But the eyes had it. Kicker Al Del Greco and Titans strength and conditioning coach Steve Watterson, standing on the sideline, alerted coach Jeff Fisher that they saw Wilkins step out of bounds in front of them. The Titans reviewed the play, and the return was brought back.

"Watterson's been around here for (14) years," linebacker Eddie Robinson said. "I've been wondering why he's been here all this time. He finally justified his stay."

And the Titans held on, advancing to the AFC Championship Game in the process. They won despite the fact quarterback Steve McNair threw for just 112 yards.

"No one gave us a chance to come in here and win," said George, who broke a franchise record for playoff rushing yards in the game. "In some ways, we like it that way. In the playoffs, it's not about dominating the other team. We just have to keep giving ourselves a chance to win games, and that's what we're doing."

DANCE PARTY

The Titans swept the regular season series from the Jaguars in 1999, but would need to beat them a third time—in Jacksonville on Jan. 24, 2000—to advance to Super Bowl XXXIV.

Again, not many gave the Titans a chance. The night before the game, Titans coach Jeff Fisher gave his players even more incentive. He showed them a clip of Jacksonville's players singing, "Uh Oh," the Jaguars' Super Bowl song.

The next day, a riled up bunch of Titans punched their Super Bowl ticket with a 33–14 win, setting the stage for a Super Bowl XXXIV showdown in Atlanta against the St. Louis Rams.

"It was very touching to see (former Oiler defensive tackle) Gary Walker singing," Titans quarterback Steve McNair said of the clip. "That was all fun and games. They were all excited. They had reason to be excited; they were playing at home and they had a great chance of winning. But somehow we spoiled that."

For Walker and the Jaguars, it was the end of road. "This game wasn't lost because of no song, no cockiness," Walker said afterward. "To make a long story short, we just went out there and got our asses kicked."

To the Titans, the game was also about much more than a clip. It was the reward for all the hard work over the previous years, and it showed in their celebration. Owner Bud

Al Del Greco connects on a field goal during the Titans' 19–16 victory over the Indianapolis Colts in the AFC Divisional Playoffs January 16, 2000. (Photo by Mary Ann Carter/NFL/Getty Images)

Adams proudly held the Lamar Hunt trophy, then passed it around to players like veteran offensive lineman Bruce Matthews, running back Eddie George, and McNair. Players didn't want to leave the field at ALLTEL Stadium.

McNair ran for two touchdowns and threw for another as the Titans rallied from a 14–10 halftime deficit. Return man Derrick Mason opened the game with an 80-yard return following a safety, and a clutch 51-yard run by McNair set up a one-yard touchdown run late that secured the win. The Titans' defense forced six Jacksonville turnovers.

"It's like a dream," a jubilant Matthews said. "It's a little bit hard to believe it's coming true like this. After all these years, I'm actually going to the Super Bowl. Can you believe this?"

BREAKOUT

The Titans became the first team in NFL history to defeat a team three times in one season while winning the final game on the road. Overall, the Titans became the eighth team to sweep another team three times in one season.

NO HOT-LANTA

The Super Bowl is known for being in a warm climate, but Atlanta, Georgia, was anything but during Super Bowl week. Many of the Titans came unprepared, without enough warm clothes. Temperatures were in the 20s during the week, with below-zero wind chills. An ice storm hit the city late in the week.

"Our guys will have pneumonia by the time it's over with," Titans general manager Floyd Reese said at the time.

The Titans players, however, took offense to the frosty reception they felt they got from the NFL. While the Rams basked inside a swanky—and heated—ballroom at their hotel, the Titans did their mandatory media sessions during the week in a poorly heated tent adjacent to their hotel. Word spread fast.

"The Rams are inside?" Titans defensive lineman Mike Jones asked. "See, we're the stepchild, we get no love."

Eventually, the Titans got more heaters in their tents. Unfortunately, they were so loud it made it difficult for coach Jeff Fisher to hear the questions from the media at his press conferences each day.

SUPER BOWL XXXIV

They belonged.

They had gone to Indianapolis and won 19–16 behind a team playoff-record 162 rushing yards from Eddie George, including a 68-yard touchdown. They had gone to Jacksonville and crushed the Jaguars 33–14, their third victory over the AFC's top-seeded team that season. Nearly everyone had played well. The defense had forced six turnovers and recorded its second safety of the playoffs. McNair had rushed for 91 yards and a pair of touchdowns on just nine carries. Derrick Mason had returned a kickoff 80 yards for a touchdown. That they had needed a miracle to get by Buffalo in the first round only made them feel as if they'd been anointed to win the NFL title. Now, they were on a roll.

"It sort of felt like team of destiny," Titans tight end Frank Wycheck said. "We were not the flashiest team but at the same time had a great year. People forget how tough the game

The Titans' amazing run through the 2000 playoffs resulted in the first Super Bowl berth in the franchise's history. (Photo by Tom Hauck/Getty Images)

against Buffalo was. They were a good team with a great defense [tops in the NFL]. You just kind of felt something after that game. Seeing Bruce [Matthews] and Marcus [Robertson] and all of those guys who were part of that 1992 game…finally it had come back around for those guys. They can forget that famous comeback by the Bills [backup quarterback Frank Reich led Buffalo back from a 38–3 third-quarter deficit against the Houston Oilers, the precursor to the Titans, in a playoff game in the 1992 season]. We had fun with it. It gives you confidence. It prepares you for anything that could come up. It lifts your confidence.

"We had no question in our minds that we could win the Super Bowl. We were confident as we could be."

The NFC champion St. Louis Rams weren't going to be pushovers. They belonged in Atlanta for Super Bowl XXXIV, too. They had come out of nowhere to go a conference-best 13–3 behind quarterback Kurt Warner, a backup and former Arena League signal-caller who got his opportunity when starter Trent Green suffered a season-ending injury during a preseason game.

The Rams had become "the greatest show on turf." Their quick-strike capability put fear in the hearts of most defenses. Warner had completed 65.1 percent of his passes for 4,353 yards, 41 touchdowns, and just 13 interceptions, making him an easy choice as the

league's Most Valuable Player. But he was far from the only weapon. Running back Marshall Faulk had 1,381 rushing yards and had 1,048 receiving yards, becoming just the second player in NFL history to accomplish the feat of 1,000 in each category in the same season (San Francisco 49ers running back Roger Craig was the other). Faulk was Warner's favorite target—he had 87 receptions—but wide receiver Isaac Bruce wasn't far behind. He hauled in 77 passes for 1,165 yards and 12 touchdowns. Torry Holt, the Rams' first-round pick and No. 6 overall, emerged opposite Bruce and finished his rookie campaign with 52 receptions for 788 yards and six touchdowns.

Lost in all of the pyrotechnics of the Rams' offense was the fact coach Dick Vermeil and his staff had fashioned a solid defense to go along with it. St. Louis had the league's best rushing defense, and the unit ranked fourth overall. It was anchored by defensive ends Kevin Carter and Grant Wistrom, linebackers London Fletcher and Mike Jones, and cornerback Todd Lyght.

The elements were present for an epic matchup. The Titans' recipe for success was to run Eddie George then run him some more, and if that didn't work Fisher would call for… Eddie George. No secrets, no gimmicks. The Titans would do it, and the Rams would be ready for it.

The Rams were installed as seven-point favorites, and the game certainly started as though the guys in Vegas knew what they were talking about. St. Louis was able to move the ball effectively in the first half. After being stymied on their first drive when Titans safety Blaine Bishop blitzed and pressured Warner into an errant third-down throw, the Rams proceeded to take the ball into the red zone on their next four possessions.

That's when the Tennessee defense rose to the occasion. The Titans were able to keep the Rams out of the end zone despite being gashed by the vertical passing attack of offensive coordinator Mike Martz. St. Louis attempted four field goals in the first 30 minutes, and Jeff Wilkins made three. He missed one from 34 yards, but still the Rams led 9–0 at the break.

Fisher didn't panic. His team had come too far and had played too well whenever adversity seemed like it was getting the best of the Titans. The score seemed like a gift when you consider the Rams had piled up 294 total yards to the Titans' paltry 89.

"We didn't play well in the first half," Fisher said. "They came out and were just slinging it all over the place and for some reason we thought because they were throwing it, we could throw it. I think we went into the locker room down 16–0 [the Rams lead did reach 16–0 but not until the third quarter]. We got in there and said, 'Hey, let's get back to what got us here,' and that's what we did."

Their determination renewed, the Titans took the second-half kickoff and drove 43 yards to the St. Louis 29. But they couldn't get on the scoreboard— Lyght blocked Al Del Greco's 47-yard field-goal attempt. That's when the Rams pushed the lead to 16. Warner completed a 31-yard pass to Bruce and a 16-yarder to tight end Ernie Conwell to propel his team down the field. He capped the 68-yard drive with a nine-yard strike to Holt as the rookie slid inside of Titans

> **We didn't play well in the first half… we went into the locker room…and said, 'Hey, let's get back to what got us here,' and that's what we did.**

Eddie George bulls for yardage against the St. Louis Rams in Super Bowl XXXIV. (Photo by Al Messerschmidt/NFL/Getty Images)

cornerback Dainon Sidney. The lead now was 16–0, and it looked as though another miracle would be needed.

Derrick Mason returned the ensuing kickoff 35 yards to the Tennessee 34. Getting back to Titans football, Fisher called George's number five times over the next seven plays, and sure enough he began to find some room. McNair also hooked up with Wycheck twice, and when McNair scrambled 23 yards to the Rams' 2, suddenly the Titans had a pulse. Two plays later George plunged in from the 1, and the lead was trimmed to 16–6. Fisher decided to go for two, but McNair's pass for Wycheck was wide and fell harmlessly to the Georgia Dome turf.

Tennessee forced St. Louis to punt on its next possession, and McNair and George went back to work. The quarterback had a pair of 21-yard completions, one to tight end Jackie Harris and the other to wide receiver Isaac Byrd, and the running back kept pounding away. The Titans covered 79 yards in 13 plays, and when George scored from two yards out and Del Greco booted the extra point, Tennessee trailed only 16–13 with 7:21 to play.

Momentum was wearing Titans colors. The defense came out fired up and held the Rams to a three-and-out. When Mike Horan got off a shaky punt that traveled only 30 yards, the Tennessee offense was back in business at its own 47. The Titans were able to penetrate to the St. Louis 26, but that's where the drive stalled. They turned to Del Greco, who nursed through a 43-yard field goal to tie the game at 16-all with just 2:12 remaining. The 16-point deficit was the largest ever to be erased in a Super Bowl.

To that point in the second half, the Titans' defense had stuffed the vaunted Rams' offense. They had erased the shaky first half from their minds and held St. Louis to just 71 yards for the first 27:48 of the second half.

But the Rams' quick-strike ability surfaced at just the right time for them, just the wrong time for the Titans. On the first play from scrimmage after Tennessee had tied the game, Warner went deep to Bruce down the right sideline. He got the ball off just as he was smacked to the turf by Jevon Kearse.

Titans cornerback Denard Walker had man-to-man coverage on Bruce, and the wide receiver beat him off the line. Walker recovered and was stride for stride with Bruce but didn't see that the ball had been underthrown. Bruce made a swim move and got underneath Walker as the ball arrived, and he caught the ball around the Titans' 38 as Walker tumbled to the turf in front of him. Bruce cut inside, and he was gone. The play covered 73 yards, and when Wilkins booted the extra point, the Rams had gone back in front, 23–16. It had happened in a matter of seconds.

"We didn't want to go to overtime, so he had to make a big play," Bruce said. "They had been in man-to-man coverage all day long, and there was no trickery. Kurt just had to make sure that he got the ball to me. And he did."

In a way, the manner in which the Rams scored was good news for the Titans, too. It's not like St. Louis had run the clock down to next-to-nothing and scored at the buzzer. There still was 1:54 to play, and the Titans hadn't come this far to give up now.

> **We didn't want to go to overtime, so he had to make a big play.... Kurt just had to make sure that he got the ball to me. And he did.**

Tennessee Titans head coach Jeff Fisher before Super Bowl XXXIV. (Photo by Allen Kee/NFL/Getty Images)

They also were hoping not to go as far as they needed to go. A holding penalty on the kickoff set the Titans back to their own 10 to start the game's final drive, but McNair hit Mason for nine yards and Wycheck for seven to provide some breathing room. After an incompletion, McNair scrambled for 12 yards, and when cornerback Dre' Bly was called for a personal foul for a facemask on the Titans' quarterback, suddenly Tennessee was in St. Louis territory and there still were 59 seconds to play.

St. Louis was penalized five yards on the next play for being offside, moving the ball to the 40. McNair ran for two yards, then he found Dyson for seven more. Three plays later, with the Titans facing a third-and-five, it was time for some McNair magic.

When he was in his prime, few quarterbacks in the history of the game could match scrambling ability with brute strength quite like McNair. He was 6'2" and 230-plus pounds, and he had thrown more than one defensive lineman off his back and stiff-armed his fair share of blitzing linebackers. As Fisher would say years later, "I'm not sure at that

time I could have called him one of the three or four best quarterbacks in the league, but in my mind he was one of the three or four best football players in the league. He found a way to make plays. That was it."

Here he was, making another unbelievable play on the game's biggest stage. McNair took a shotgun snap and started to scramble right, then swung back around toward the pocket. Flushed by Rams defensive end Jay Williams, McNair was forced right again, where defensive end Kevin Carter was waiting. Somehow he ran out of the grasp of Carter as Williams lunged, too. Williams nearly got him around the collar, and Carter had a handful of jersey as he fell to the turf, trying to pull McNair down with him. The quarterback put his left hand down and somehow kept his balance as the two behemoths landed on each other while he ran forward and out of harm's way. He looked up and fired to Dyson, who had taken advantage of all of the time McNair had bought to work his way open around the Rams' 13. He was tackled at the 10, and the Titans used their final timeout with six seconds remaining.

It was the kind of situation you dream about as a kid from almost the first time you pick up a football: One play from 10 yards out to be in position to win the Super Bowl. The Titans had covered 80 yards in 1:48, but it all would mean little unless they could punch it in now.

"It was a man-tight and zone-side call," Dyson said. "I went in motion to identify the coverage. It went from my motion. McNair knew and I knew he knew he was coming to me. Frank was the decoy, a clearout, and I was coming underneath him."

"I was one of the primary reads," Wycheck said. "We had run the play in the previous game and I had caught a touchdown. Steve kind of read the safeties and read underneath coverage and could go front side. He made the right read.

"I wanted 3-over-2 coverage, zone. He [Rams linebacker Mike Jones] ran with me for a couple of steps and he peeled off and sensed Kevin coming underneath. There was a corner and a safety over the top, which took the seam out of the read for Steve. He got off me right away. He saw Jones turn with me for a couple of steps. Steve made the right throw."

The throw was a slant to Dyson, who had sneaked in underneath Wycheck as he tried to take as many defenders as possible deeper and into the end zone with him. Jones turned just in time and was able to get his right hand on Dyson's right thigh pad and then wrap up around the receiver's legs. Dyson reached the ball out with his right hand for the goal line, but he was one yard short.

"When I saw that ball go in the air, I said, 'It's a touchdown.' I was ready to call coach Martz and tell him to get the script ready for overtime," Vermeil said.

Alas, the Titans had run out of miracles.

"I think in those situations with the clock and things like that you hurry some things," Fisher said. "Had Kevin gone a couple of yards deeper he would have caught the ball in the end zone. Mike would have flipped his hips up the field and not been able to come back and make the play. But that's the game."

"To come this far and be a half-yard short is just a sick feeling," Dyson said. "When he got his hands on me, I thought I'd break the tackle. But he slid down to my foot, like you're supposed to, and made a great play. I realized as soon as I stretched out and was going down that I didn't get the point of the ball over the goal line."

Simply put, Jones had made a great play. He called it the biggest of his career, and he was right. "When you're a little kid, you dream about scoring touchdowns, not stopping

Kevin Dyson's reach for the end zone on the final play of Super Bowl XXXIV ended up just inches short, bringing the Titans' dreams of a championship to an end. (Photo by Kevin Reece/NFL/Getty Images)

them," Jones said. "I just grabbed him, held on, and fell down. When I looked up the clock said zero-zero and we had won the Super Bowl."

"I knew my man Mike would be there," St. Louis middle linebacker London Fletcher said. "I just looked up at the clock, the clock was at zero. I didn't know what to do. It was the ultimate feeling—relief, jubilation, fatigue. It was quite a moment."

> *To come this far and be a half-yard short is just a sick feeling.*

Fisher said that had Dyson scored he would have kicked the extra point and gone to overtime because he felt like his team had the momentum. "They were dead tired," Fisher said of the Rams.

All of the Titans took the loss hard, especially McNair and Dyson. "I don't ever want to feel like this again," McNair said. "We were able to get some Super Bowl experience. When we come back the next time, we'll feel more comfortable. We're only going to get better."

Dyson was devastated, from the highest of highs at the Music City Miracle to the lowest of lows, coming up a yard short in the Super Bowl. "That's the epitome of football," Dyson said. "I had never in my athletic life experienced something like the Super Bowl. I'd experienced game-winning catches in football and game-winning baskets in basketball and game-winning goals in soccer. Nothing matched up to the miracle. Now here was the biggest game of my life, my number was called, and I wasn't successful. It was the biggest bitter pill you could swallow."

The bitterness subsided somewhat from a strange source. Dyson did a couple of interviews after the season with Jones, both of them discussing one of the most exciting finishes in Super Bowl history. "To hear his explanation and how humble he was.... He said it could have gone either way. I didn't say it, he said it. 'If I hadn't reached back and seen Kevin when I did....' He was very humble.

"Mike and I have had a friendship since then. We're always going to be linked. To hear his take, I was pleased to say the least. It made me more comfortable. It made it a little easier to take."

Fisher still has vivid memories of the postgame happenings and the days after the game. He recalls thinking during the press conference that followed the game that he wanted to go find Vermeil because he hadn't had a chance to shake his hand after the game. Fisher caught up to the Rams' coach in the victors' locker room. But not before the Titans coach's press conference was interrupted so he could take a phone call.

TITANS TIDBITS FROM '99

The Titans were 10–1 when they won the coin toss....The Titans were 8–0 when they scored on their first drive....The Titans were 12–0 when they won the turnover battle.... The Titans were 10–0 when they led at halftime....The Titans averaged 5.3 yards per play on first down, which ranked second in the AFC....The Titans were 13–1 when they scored 20 or more points and 11–1 when they allowed 20 or fewer points.

"Vice President Gore (a Tennessee native) wanted to congratulate me on a great game," Fisher said. "It was a great conversation. I'll never forget it. Then the press conference was over, and initially the security guys weren't going to let my boys in the locker room. We finally get in, and I'm getting ready to take a shower, just kind of sitting there. Two guys come in and say, 'You need to take a phone call.' I said, 'I'm done taking phone calls.' 'No, the president is gonna call on the phone outside.' I said, 'What president?' They said, 'President Clinton.' So I go out and have a conversation with him. He says, 'We had whole group here at the Oval Office watching, and you should be proud.' I almost felt like saying, 'Well, Mr. President, we lost.' But those things…you reflect back. It took me a good week and then you're off and running again. It just starts again."

The Titans' spirits were lifted after the game by the fans. It was a season worth celebrating, not focusing on how close they had come in the Super Bowl.

"The parade experience was incredible, the reception we got here," Fisher said. "I'll never forget a poster that a woman was holding as the parade route was ending, it said, 'A setback is a setup for a comeback.' That's kind of what carried us through that. I made the comment publicly and I got a letter from this woman and a copy of a book that was titled just that. And basically it said your comeback is already taking place. That's kind of how we handled that off-season."

Fisher said he still hasn't watched Super Bowl XXXIV. "I saw it in person. I don't need to see it," the coach said. "We don't need motivating factors, but it's an additional motivating factor.

The Titans made it back to the playoffs three of the next four seasons with the core of McNair, George, Wycheck and Bruce Matthews on offense, and Kearse and cornerback Samari Rolle on defense. But they've yet to reach another Super Bowl.

"This game…coaches always use the phrase 'a game of inches,' and it is," Fisher said. "Three or four inches either way in the replay (in the Music City Miracle), a handful of inches on the last play in the Super Bowl. You can't dwell on those things as you move through your coaching career.

"We got to experience both sides. The positive side is what happens when the replay official says on the field, 'The play stands,' everything in the locker room afterward and all the momentum. The other side of it is it's just over and you have to come to terms with that."

> **Coaches always use the phrase 'a game of inches,' and it is.**

Fisher has come to terms with the loss, but he'll never make peace with it. He will be driven to win a championship until he does, and he'll be driven to win a second once he bags his first. If and when he does he'll do it without 1999 cornerstones McNair and George, both of whom have since retired. McNair ran for 64 yards, a Super Bowl record for quarterbacks. George had 95 yards and two touchdowns on 28 carries. Oddly enough, it was the first time the Titans had ever lost when George carried at least 27 times (15-1).

"Wednesday after the parade and post wrapup meetings were all over with, Eddie came into my office," Fisher said. "He said, 'Coach, I don't want to go the Pro Bowl.' I said, 'Eddie, are you crazy? What are you talking about?' He had to get on a plane and go. He said, 'I don't want to go.' I said, 'Eddie, it's a chance to go and unwind and play with the best players in the league and be recognized.' And he said, 'Jeff, I want to get started on next season right now, here, today.' That was what the whole experience did for this organization. That was the attitude moving forward."

THANKS, TITANS

Parades are usually reserved for champions.

But two days after the Titans' heartbreaking loss to the St. Louis Rams in Super Bowl XXXIV, the city of Nashville wanted to celebrate what was a magical season and say "Thanks."

An estimated 60,000 fans turned out on a cold February day, lining Broadway and Second Avenue North. Fans hung out windows of buildings, while others cheered on from rooftops.

All the while, for more than an hour, fans at the Coliseum waited for their heroes to arrive, bundling up in blankets and watching a live broadcast of the approaching parade on the scoreboard video screens. Titans coach Jeff Fisher and his players rode in convertibles and were showered in confetti in near-freezing temperatures as the parade route went through downtown. Fans slapped high-fives with their favorite players. It was a moment to remember.

"We're going to go back there next year and make sure we win it," Fisher told the crowd. Then, with a smile, he quoted a sign he saw along the parade route: "A setback is just a setup for a comeback."

AWARDS

Titans defensive end Jevon Kearse busted on the scene in his rookie season in 1999, impacting the game like few rookies have ever done.

Kearse, the 16th pick of the 1999 draft, set an NFL rookie record with 14.5 sacks and at the end of the season was named NFL Defensive Rookie of the Year by the Associated Press, earning 49 of the 50 votes by a media panel.

"I wanted to show all the teams that passed me up…that they missed out and I think I did a pretty good job of stating that," Kearse said. "I shouldn't have fallen to the 16th pick, but I'm actually glad it happened…. In the back of my head, I'm just laughing at some other teams."

Kearse also recorded 59 tackles forced 10 fumbles in '99.

Aside from Kearse, three other Titans were rewarded with trips to the Pro Bowl after the 1999 season—running back Eddie George, tight end Frank Wycheck, and offensive lineman Bruce Matthews.

RSTS IN TITANS ERAFIRSTS IN TITANS ERAFIRSTS IN TITANS ERAFIRSTS IN TITANS ERAFIRSTS IN TITANS ERAFIRSTS IN TITANS ERAFIRSTS IN TITANS ER

FIRSTS IN TITANS ERA, achieved in 1999 season

First preseason victory: vs. Atlanta, 17–3 (8/27/99)

First regular season victory: vs. Cincinnati, 36–35 (9/12/99)

First touchdown: Steve McNair 1-yard run vs. Cincinnati (9/12/99)

First touchdown run: Steve McNair 1-yard run vs. Cincinnati (9/12/99)

First touchdown reception: Kevin Dyson, 13 yards from McNair vs. Cincinnati (9/12/99)

First field goal: Al Del Greco, 50 yards vs. Cincinnati (9/12/99)

First game-winning field goal: Al Del Greco, 33 yards vs. Cincinnati (9/12/99)

First tackle: Blaine Bishop, Marcus Robertson on Corey Dillon vs. Cincinnati (9/12/99)

First sack: Marcus Robertson, Barron Wortham on Jeff Blake vs. Cincinnati (9/12/99)

First fumble recovery: Mike Jones vs. Cleveland (9/19/99)

First forced fumble: John Thornton vs. Cleveland (9/19/99)

First safety: Donald Mitchell blocked punt of Will Brice vs. Cincinnati (9/12/99)

First blocked punt: Donald Mitchell blocked punt of Will Brice vs. Cincinnati (9/12/99)

First interception: Denard Walker vs. Cincinnati (9/12/99)

First interception return for TD: Donald Mitchell, 42 yards @ New Orleans (10/17/99)

First 300-yard passing game: Steve McNair vs. Cincinnati, 341 yards (9/12/99)

First 100-yard receiving game: Kevin Dyson vs. Cincinnati, 162 yards (9/12/99)

First 100-yard rushing game: Eddie George @ New Orleans, 155 yards (10/17/99)

First sellout: vs. Cincinnati, 65,904 (9/12/99)

First playoff win: vs. Buffalo, 22–16 (1/8/00)

RSTS IN TITANS ERAFIRSTS IN TITANS ERAFIRSTS IN TITANS ERAFIRSTS IN TITANS ERAFIRSTS IN TITANS ERAFIRSTS IN TITANS ERAFIRSTS IN TITANS E

GREATEST GAMES

by Jim Wyatt

TITANS 23, STEELERS 20
Date: September 24, 2000
Site: Three Rivers Stadium, Pittsburgh

As things turned out, it didn't really matter who started at quarterback in the Titans' final game at Three Rivers Stadium, because Steve McNair finished.

Boy, did he.

No one gave a hurting McNair much of a chance to play against the Pittsburgh Steelers in Week 4, not after he was knocked out of the previous game against Kansas City with a bruised sternum. Even after a bye week, it was debatable how much McNair improved during his time off, considering he was still having trouble breathing just days before the game in Pittsburgh. He didn't practice for two weeks leading up to the game. So the Titans opted to play it safe. They decided to let back-up Neil O'Donnell start and planned to give McNair the day off.

Derrick Mason fields a kick during the Titans' 23–20 victory over the Pittsburgh Steelers on September 24, 2000. (Rick Stewart/Allsport/Getty Images)

For a while, it looked like the Titans would win without McNair. They led 13–6 after three quarters, getting a 20-yard touchdown run from running back Eddie George early, along with a pair of field goals from kicker Al Del Greco. But disaster struck not long after the Steelers rallied to take a 20–16 lead on a five-yard touchdown run by Jerome Bettis. Or so everyone thought.

With O'Donnell in the game, the Titans took over at their own 37-yard line, needing a touchdown drive to win it. But O'Donnell was knocked to the ground by Steelers linebacker Jason Gildon on a big hit. His lip was bloodied, and his head was in the clouds with a concussion. The crowd at Three Rivers Stadium was roaring, waving Terrible Towels and thirsty for more blood as George helped O'Donnell, a former Steeler, to the sideline.

Enter McNair. After spending the first 57 minutes, 25 seconds of the game as a spectator in a baseball cap, jacket and headset, McNair grabbed a football, tossed a few warm-up passes and headed to the huddle. "I don't know if he was supposed to play or not supposed to play," Steelers defensive end Kevin Henry said. "But we had things under control, and then (McNair) came in and won the game for them."

Yes he did.

McNair only threw three passes that day. He completed all of them for 55 yards, including a 22-yard completion to receiver Chris Sanders on a third-and-11 play—his first throw of the game. A few moments later, McNair's 18-yard touchdown pass to tight end Erron Kinney gave the Titans a 23–20 lead and the win. Steelers kicker Kris Brown missed a 50-yard field goal with 30 seconds remaining that would have forced overtime.

"The guys needed me," McNair said. "I wanted to play, so when I got my chance I was ready."

Several Titans could hardly believe what they witnessed at the end, especially after seeing McNair in pain for two weeks straight. It was the sign of more things to come for McNair.

"That," cornerback Samari Rolle said, "is a storybook ending."

TITANS OVER JAGS IN MONDAY NIGHT FOOTBALL DEBUT

TITANS 27, JAGUARS 13
Date: October 16, 2000
Site: The Coliseum

The Titans and Nashville debuted on *Monday Night Football* against the rival Jacksonville Jaguars, and what an impressive performance it turned out to be. On offense, the Titans ran over the Jaguars, who were hoping to exact some revenge after being swept in three games the previous season. On defense, the Titans came up with some crucial stops. It was a recipe for a Monday night celebration.

"I think we've got their number now," Titans linebacker Eddie Robinson said.

The Titans' fifth straight win over the Jaguars came before a record crowd at the stadium. Running back Eddie George ran for 165 yards and a touchdown on 30 carries, and quarterback Steve McNair threw touchdown passes to tight end Frank Wycheck and receiver Derrick Mason as the Titans jumped ahead 17–3 by halftime. A 19-yard touchdown run by George made it 24–3, and fans spent the rest of the night partying under the lights.

Titans defensive back Denard Walker brings down a Jacksonville receiver during the Titans' 27–13 victory over the Jaguars on October 16, 2000. (Andy Lyons/Allsport/Getty Images)

But not everyone was convinced, though that hardly came as a surprise to the Titans. After the game, a stubborn Fred Taylor, Jacksonville's star running back, was once again unwilling to give the Titans credit. Just like he did following all three losses to the Titans the previous year, he failed to acknowledge the Titans as the better team.

"I still think we're better," said Taylor, who rushed for 112 yards in the game. "I know it sounds stupid, and it will keep sounding stupid until we beat them."

The Titans thought their play spoke for itself. Taylor's post-game spiel only added to the rivalry. "You expect them to say, 'We just didn't play well, we're just in a skid,'" Titans tackle Brad Hopkins said. "If it was any different, it wouldn't be them. If they conceded we're the better team, it just wouldn't be Jacksonville, would it?"

TITANS WIN AT WASHINGTON ON *MONDAY NIGHT FOOTBALL*

TITANS 27, REDSKINS 21
Date: October 30, 2000
Site: FedEx Field, Washington, D.C.

Redskins fans dressed up in Halloween costumes before a "Monday Night Football" audience, while the Titans dressed up like magicians and pulled one out of a hat.

They managed to win a game when they were far from their best in large part because of some remarkable—and improbable—plays. How crazy was it? Well, the Titans had a 20–7 lead at halftime without a touchdown from their offense, which managed just five first downs in the first 30 minutes.

Linebacker Eddie Robinson tries to keep Washington's Larry Centers out of the end zone during the Titans' 27–21 victory October 30, 2000. (Doug Pensinger/Allsport/Getty Images)

Longtime Titans fans probably remember how they did it. One touchdown came on a 69-yard punt return from Derrick Mason, who fielded the punt and after initially heading right, cut up the middle and raced to the end zone.

"Once I got through the first wave…it was just me and the kicker," Mason said. "I knew I couldn't get tackled by the kicker."

Mason didn't. The touchdown gave the Titans a 10–7 lead with 11:12 remaining in the second quarter, and it ignited a 17–0 scoring spurt to close out the half.

"I think that return was key to us winning the game," linebacker Keith Bulluck, who provided a key block on the return, said. "That sparked us, and sent them a message that we could strike anywhere, not just with No. 27 [Eddie George], or No. 9 [Steve McNair] or No. 89 [Frank Wycheck]. We have a lot of weapons on this team."

Bulluck failed to mention No. 21—cornerback Samari Rolle, who managed to outdo Mason right before the half in one of the NFL's most memorable plays of the 2000 season. On the final play of the first half, with the Titans clinging to a 13–7 lead, Rolle intercepted Redskins quarterback Brad Johnson at the Titans' 19-yard line and proceeded to put on a show.

Frank Wycheck fights to hang onto the ball as he is tackled by Brian Dawkins of the Philadelphia Eagles on December 3, 2000. (Harry How/Allsport/Getty Images)

He returned the interception 81 yards for a touchdown. Almost every Redskins player on the field had a chance to bring Rolle down, but he somehow managed to make it into the end zone before being mobbed by his teammates.

"I was winded when I got all the way," said Rolle, who had two interceptions in the game. "I was just fortunate to make a play."

The touchdown gave the Titans a 20–7 halftime lead despite being outgained 142 to 71 yards on offense. They held on in the second half, getting an 18-yard touchdown catch from Wycheck, to improve to 7–1 at the season's halfway point.

"It's like the rule now instead of the exception," veteran Bruce Matthews said. "We know, somehow, we'll find a way."

DEL GRECO KICKS FIVE FIELD GOALS
TITANS 15, EAGLES 13
Date: December 3, 2000
Site: Veterans Stadium, Philadelphia

Titans kicker Al Del Greco was a man on the spot. But on a sub-freezing day in the City of Brotherly Love, he also ended up being the man on his teammates' shoulders after kicking the game-winner to beat the Eagles. It sure beat being a goat.

After falling behind 13–12 with 3 minutes, 11 seconds left in the game when Eagles quarterback Donovan McNabb scored the game's only touchdown on a two-yard run, the Titans needed a drive and another kick.

Quarterback Steve McNair, playing on a sprained ankle, moved the Titans 32 yards down the field to get Del Greco into field-goal range, completing key passes to Derrick Mason, Chris Sanders, Eddie George, and Frank Wycheck along the way.

"It's like the norm around here," Mason said. "We know if we get into a two-minute situation, Steve's going to do what he has to make us win."

But Del Greco had to do his part, too, which hadn't been a given in previous weeks. Del Greco was under scrutiny heading into the contest for missing an extra point and a decisive 43-yard kick against the Baltimore Ravens three weeks earlier, plus a 28-yarder late in the game the previous week in a loss at Jacksonville.

On this day, Del Greco came through, time and again. His 50-yard field goal sailed through the uprights as time expired to give the Titans the dramatic 15–13 win over the Eagles. On the day, Del Greco, in his 17th NFL season, made a personal-record five field goals, hitting earlier from 26, 42, 22, and 44 yards. Some of his teammates admittedly closed their eyes on the last one, too nervous to watch.

"He put all that stuff behind him, refocused himself on what he had to do and put 15 points on the board," tackle Brad Hopkins said. "That's more than two touchdowns—enough said."

It was instant relief for Del Greco, who scored the team's only points that blustery day at Veterans Stadium. "Awesome," Del Greco said. "It's always more fun when it's THE last play of the game and you don't have to kick off.…What was there, six seconds? It was a long enough field goal that the time expired while it was in the air. It was a good feeling."

TITANS GRIND OUT BLIZZARD WIN
TITANS 24, BROWNS 0
Date: December 17, 2000
Site: Cleveland Browns Stadium, Cleveland

In blizzard-like conditions, Titans running back Eddie George ran like a snowplow in one of the coldest games in franchise history.

Temperature at kickoff in Cleveland was 20 degrees with a wind chill off Lake Erie of minus-10. Winds gusted up to 30 miles an hour, and at the start of the second half the temperature was 7 degrees with a wind-chill of minus-18. Heavy snow and ice pelted the players throughout, leaving the ground covered.

"Usually when it snows it's a little bit warmer," George said. "But the combination of snow and a vicious wind chill—it was like a razor blade out there."

George, however, didn't seem to mind a bit. He switched to longer cleats to get a better grip on the snow-covered field, then sliced through Cleveland's defense in a 24–0 win. He ended up rushing for 176 yards and three touchdowns in the game.

"It seems like the worse the conditions," tackle Fred Miller said, "the better he gets."

On defense, the Titans held the Browns to just six first downs and 113 total yards for the organization's first shutout in 115 games, dating back seven seasons. Afterward, however, few players stuck around long on the field to celebrate. In fact, it was so cold before the game, some players decided to skip warm-ups.

"Coach (Jeff) Fisher mentioned that was probably the fastest ever a team got back to the locker room after a ball game," defensive tackle Joe Salave'a said with a smile. "But who could blame us?"

Eddie George and the Titans overcame blizzard-like conditions during a 24–0 victory over the Cleveland Browns on December 17, 2000. (Jamie Squire/Allsport/Getty Images)

Even Fisher couldn't.

"We went through five gallons of chicken bouillon on the sideline and there were a lot of guys I didn't recognize in those jackets," Fisher said. "But I was impressed. We talk about going out there with bare arms and just playing and we had a lot of guys doing that."

CHRISTMAS NIGHT, 2000
TITANS 31, COWBOYS 0
Date: December 25, 2000
Site: The Coliseum

So much was on the line for the Titans when the Dallas Cowboys came to town on Christmas night during the 2000 season.

Yancey Thigpen battles for a pass against Mario Edwards of the Dallas Cowboys during the Titans' 31–0 victory over Dallas on December 25, 2000. (Jamie Squire/Allsport/Getty Images)

The Titans were trying to earn a first-round playoff bye, along with a chance to finish with the NFL's top-ranked defense. And, once again, their reputation was on the line as the *Monday Night Football* cameras put them in the spotlight. The Titans took full advantage in one of the most dominating defensive performances in franchise history.

The Titans held Dallas to just 95 yards of total offense and overtook the Baltimore Ravens to finish the year as the league's top defense. It was the team's second straight shutout on defense after blanking the Browns the previous week. Their 13–3 finish tied their mark from the previous season.

"We wanted to come out and make a statement as a defense and show teams to come we are nothing to mess around with," said defensive lineman Henry Ford, who picked up a fumble and rumbled 30 yards for a touchdown in the second half, when the Titans blew the game open. "To get two goose eggs in a row, that's a blessing."

Dallas managed only six first downs in the game, as quarterback Anthony Wright completed 5 of 20 passes for 35 yards and was picked off twice and sacked four times.

As a rookie, Titans linebacker Keith Bulluck first began to earn the nickname he later created for himself—"Mr. Monday Night." Bulluck intercepted a pass in the third quarter and returned it eight yards for a touchdown. He'd eventually make a habit of making big plays in "MNF" games.

Quarterback Steve McNair threw for 188 yards in the game, and running back Eddie George rushed for 83 yards to eclipse the 1,500-yard mark for the season. The victory allowed the Titans to claim their first AFC Central Division crown since 1993, and with their league-best record they also earned a first-round bye. The shutout marked the only time in franchise history that the team recorded shutouts in consecutive games.

Skip Hicks carries the ball during the Titans 13–10 victory over the Oakland Raiders on December 22, 2001. (Jonathan Ferrey/Getty Images)

The Titans weren't able to take advantage of home-field advantage in the playoffs, however. After the bye, they ended up losing their opening playoff game 24–10 at the Coliseum to the Baltimore Ravens, who went on to win Super Bowl XXXV.

LAST-MINUTE FIELD GOAL PROVIDES WIN OVER OAKLAND

TITANS 13, RAIDERS 10
Date: December 22, 2001
Site: Network Associates Coliseum, Oakland

In what turned out to be a season to forget, the Titans' win in Oakland in Week 15 was at least one to remember.

On the verge of playoff elimination, the Titans showed they still had some fight in pulling out a 13–10 win over the Raiders. The decisive points came on a 21-yard field goal from kicker Joe Nedney with just 1:47 remaining in the contest, capping a 12-play, 74-yard drive that began at their own 23 with just 5:54 remaining. The win got the Titans to the .500 mark for the first—and only—time all year.

Raiders kicker Sebastian Janikowski had a chance to tie the game, but he missed his third field-goal attempt of the night in the final seconds as the Titans surprised the playoff-bound Raiders. "We haven't gotten a lot of breaks this year, and I think our guys deserved this," coach Jeff Fisher said. "This was a big game for us."

On a nationally televised game on ABC, Nedney proved to be the hero, although it was quarterback Steve McNair who once again proved gutsy just by being able to play. McNair

Frank Wycheck prepares to take on a tackler during the Titans' 27–24 victory over the Philadelphia Eagles on September 9, 2002. (Photo by Elsa/Getty Images)

was slowed all week with a bad back, and was even forced to stand up most of the way on the cross-country flight to California. He ended up completing 15 of 27 passes for 178 yards and a 30-yard touchdown strike to receiver Kevin Dyson.

Unfortunately for the Titans, they were eliminated from playoff contention the next day.

TITANS WIN 2002 SEASON OPENER OVER PHILLY
TITANS 27, EAGLES 24
Date: September 9, 2002
Site: The Coliseum

After finishing the previous season with a 7–9 mark, the Titans—and their fans—were in need of an emotional boost at the start of the 2002 season. The season opener against the Philadelphia Eagles provided just that, even though it ended up proving costly on a sweltering day at the Coliseum.

The visiting Eagles jumped out to a 24–10 lead in what was a nightmarish first half for the Titans. On just the second play of the season, they lost defensive end Jevon Kearse with a broken left foot, an injury that would end up limiting him the rest of the season.

But the Titans showed some spunk under adversity, offering a sign of things to come. A 47-yard field goal by kicker Joe Nedney in the third quarter cut Philadelphia's lead to 24–13, and then the Titans sliced the lead to 24–19 on a two-yard pass from quarterback Steve McNair to receiver Justin McCareins.

On the defensive side of the ball, the previously unknown rookie who replaced Kearse—defensive end Carlos Hall—was making a name for himself. Hall sacked Eagles quarterback Donovan McNabb three times in the game, as the Titans refused to die.

Making their comeback attempt even more difficult was the temperature, which rose to the mid-80s and forced countless players to the locker room in need of intravenous fluids. In the end, however, the Titans mustered up the strength to finish the rally, outscoring the Eagles 17–0 in the second half to win.

The decisive points came on a two-yard touchdown run by Eddie George, capping a 14-play, 84-yard drive. The two-point conversion that followed made it 27–24.

"Last year, if we were down 24–10 at halftime, you can start the bus. It's time to go," cornerback Samari Rolle said. "It's a different team now. At halftime we just said, 'Last year is done with. Let's play football.' The thing you love about this team is that nobody ever complained. We didn't quit. And we fought back."

Said defensive tackle Henry Ford: "Good teams never give up. I think we are a good team this year, and after (this game) I think that even more."

For the '02 Titans, things would end up getting worse before they got better. They ended up losing their next four games to start 1–4 before rolling off wins in 10 of their final 11 games to make the playoffs.

GOAL-LINE STAND LIFTS TITANS OVER BENGALS

TITANS 30, BENGALS 24
Date: October 27, 2002
Site: Paul Brown Stadium, Cincinnati

They say it's a game of inches. The Titans' 30–24 win in Cincinnati proved it. As things turned out, they ended up winning by a few blades of grass.

Leading in the closing moments, the Titans used a goal-line stand to hold off the Bengals, winning the game when they stopped running back Corey Dillon on a controversial fourth-down play.

"We survived," safety Lance Schulters said. "Luckily, I say luckily, we got out of here with a win."

After a back-and-forth fourth quarter, the game came down to one final play—a fourth-and-1 with 1:18 left to play. The Bengals snapped the ball, and quarterback Jon Kitna spun around and handed the ball off to Dillon, who was supposed to run through a hole in the middle. But Bengals left guard Matt O'Dwyer, who was pulling on the play, tripped, and Dillon then stumbled over O'Dwyer as he lunged for the goal line.

Titans defensive tackle Robaire Smith and linebacker Keith Bulluck were there to finish him off, but not before Dillon argued he got in. Officials ruled he didn't, and an official review said replays were inconclusive after some tense minutes of waiting. "They're officials, we're Cincinnati," Dillon said. "We don't get a call.... I thought I got it."

The Titans defense celebrated wildly twice—initially after the stop and then when the replay failed to overturn the call on the field. The Bengals had a first-and-goal from the 9, but couldn't get the touchdown in four plays.

"I knew we had them stopped because I came in at the end and my forearm was right there at the goal line and the ball was in front of my forearm," Bulluck said. "If I am a coach, I am going to do exactly what they did—go with my bread and butter. But

Justin McCareins breaks away for a big gain against the Cincinnati Bengals on October 27, 2002. The Titans won the game, 30–24. (Photo by Andy Lyons/Getty Images)

noooo.... Yeah, we are sneaking out of here with a win, but shhhh, don't tell nobody. We'll take it."

The Titans improved to 3–4 with the victory, which was part of a streak of 10 wins in their final 11 games in '02.

MCNAIR PAINFULLY GUIDES OVERTIME WIN AT GIANTS

TITANS 32, N.Y. GIANTS 29 (OT)
Date: December 1, 2002
Site: The Meadowlands, New York

During his days with the Titans, quarterback Steve McNair proved time and time again he was willing—and capable—of playing in pain. But what McNair did on a blustery December day at the Meadowlands in 2002 ranks as one of the defining moments of his career.

McNair didn't practice all week leading up to the game against the Giants because of a rib injury and a bad case of turf toe. He was in so much pain, in fact, he didn't throw a football the entire week. So when McNair took the field in warm-ups just prior to the game and was able to throw only a few short tosses, most figured he wouldn't play. His first attempt was so painful he was ready to head back to the locker room.

"I really didn't know if I was going to play or not," McNair said.

But McNair, as he did so many times in the past, took a pain-killing injection for his ribs. A hole had to be cut in the top of his shoe to make his toe more comfortable. Then McNair went out and threw for 334 yards and three touchdowns as the Titans put up a furious rally to beat the Giants in overtime, 32–29.

Joe Nedney kicks the game-winning field goal in overtime as the Titans defeated the New York Giants 32–29 on December 1, 2002. (Matt Campbell/AFP/Getty Images)

"I would say he's the toughest guy I've ever been around," guard Zach Piller said. "I figure if I look up and he's still got two arms and two legs, he's going to find a way to play."

McNair winced in pain as he crossed the goal line on a two-point conversion to tie the contest at 29–29 with just :09 left, and he had to switch the football from his right hand to his left hand so he could raise it into the air in celebration. The pain-killing shot on the right side had worn off.

Moments before, he had thrown a nine-yard touchdown pass to tight end Frank Wycheck, capping a 12-play, 81-yard drive in the closing minutes. The Titans won it in overtime on a 38-yard field goal from kicker Joe Nedney.

"I always want to play," McNair said. "If you're going to be a leader, you have to put it out on the field. I tried to do that."

It was a remarkable win for the Titans all-around. They trailed 26–14 early in the fourth quarter when Giants running back Tiki Barber scored on a one-yard touchdown run. A one-yard run by Titans running back Eddie George cut the lead to 26–21, and then the Titans got a big stop from their defense, which kept the Giants out of the end zone after they had a first-and-goal at the 1.

Barber was stopped on consecutive handoffs before Giants quarterback Kerry Collins threw an incompletion. The Giants then had to settle for a field goal for a 29–21 lead, which kept the Titans in position to tie the score with some late-game heroics. The win improved the Titans to 7–5, keeping their playoff hopes alive.

"If we had lost this game, we'd have been on life support, looking for help," defensive tackle John Thornton said. "We'd have been looking for some kind of donor or something."

WILD WIN OVER PITTSBURGH IN 2002 PLAYOFFS
TITANS 34, STEELERS 31 (OT)
Date: January 11, 2003
Site: The Coliseum

Herman Boone saw something coming, but even he never could have envisioned what happened when the Titans squared off against the Pittsburgh Steelers in a wild playoff game.

As the Titans held their team meeting the night before their AFC Divisional Playoff Game against the Steelers, coach Jeff Fisher wanted to add an extra piece of motivation. He dimmed the lights in a meeting room at the team hotel, and the players watched an eight-to 10-minute clip from the movie, *Remember the Titans*. When the lights came back on, there was Boone, the high school coach who was the inspiration for the movie. Instantly, the room was buzzing.

"He told us we were going to win because we were Titans," defensive tackle John Thornton recalled. "That kind of gave everybody goose bumps. He told us the game was going to be close, we were going to trade scores and we were going to win at the end."

With Boone watching from the sideline, the Titans pulled off the unthinkable. If you don't believe it, just ask the Steelers. The Titans beat the Steelers 34–31 in overtime in one of the craziest and most memorable games ever played at the Coliseum. The winning points came on a 26-yard field goal by kicker Joe Nedney, who had to kick the ball three times before one counted.

Nedney's first kick sailed through the uprights, prompting fireworks, but it didn't count because the Steelers had called time out. He kicked it again minutes later but missed.

Robert Holcombe runs with the ball in the Titans' 34–31 overtime victory against the Pittsburgh Steelers in the 2003 playoffs. (Photo by Scott Boehm/Getty Images)

This time, Steelers cornerback Dwayne Washington was called for running into the kicker. Then came the game-winner for Nedney, who had misfired on a 48-yarder on the final play of regulation.

"The dream that I had wasn't quite like what happened," Nedney said. "It ended right, but it was crazy."

The Steelers didn't go quietly, and grew even more incensed in the hours that followed the game after Nedney kidded that he "might try acting" after his football career ends, insinuating he exaggerated when he fell down after Washington brushed him. "He was fake falling," an upset Washington said. "Kickers are taught to do that."

Either way, it was a remarkable win for the Titans, who got 338 passing yards and two touchdowns from quarterback Steve McNair. Eddie George was knocked out of the contest with a concussion. "Nobody knew how we were going to do it, but I think everybody on the team knew that we would find a way to win," safety Lance Schulters said. "I just had a feeling it was going to come down to a field goal and we were going to make it."

Titans wide receiver Tyrone Calico tries to break free of Houston defensive back Marcus Coleman's grasp during Tennessee's 38–17 victory over the Texans on October 12, 2003. (Photo by Elsa/Getty Images)

The Titans ended up losing to the Raiders 41–24 the following week in the AFC Championship Game in Oakland, ending their 2002 season.

MCNAIR HAS RECORD-SETTING DAY IN WIN OVER HOUSTON

TITANS 38, TEXANS 17
Date: October 12, 2003
Site: The Coliseum

As Titans quarterback Steve McNair built his case for NFL co-MVP honors in 2003, his performance against the Houston Texans in Week 6 was probably marked "Exhibit A." As far as dramatic endings go, the Titans' 38–17 win over the Texans doesn't qualify among the top in team annals. McNair's day, however, was one to remember.

He threw for a career-high 421 yards and three touchdowns in the contest, drawing a standing ovation from the home crowd as coach Jeff Fisher sent back-up quarterback Billy Volek in to handle the game's final snap. "I didn't know what was going on," McNair said of the late-game substitution. "That was great, and one of those moments you don't see often in the NFL because every game seems to be tight.… It was a great feeling to come off the field and have everyone give you a standing ovation."

McNair threw all three touchdowns to receiver Derrick Mason. A 32-yard touchdown to Mason early made it 7–0. Not long after, McNair and Mason connected again for a 46-

Rocky Calmus (54) is congratulated by teammates Peter Sirmon (59) and Kevin Carter (93) after Calmus intercepted a pass from Byron Leftwich of the Jacksonville Jaguars in the Titans' 10–3 victory on November 16, 2003. (Photo by Elsa/Getty Images)

yard score. In the fourth quarter, McNair and Mason did it again, pairing up for a 50-yard strike. Mason had six catches for 177 yards in the game.

"This is the best I've seen him play," Texans coach Dom Capers said. "His experience is really paying off. Earlier in his career, he was much quicker to take the ball down and run with it. Now he can do more things with the ball."

McNair maxed out with a 158.3 quarterback rating in the first half, and completed 12 straight passes during one stretch. He ended with a QB rating of 146.8. The Titans also got a 51-yard interception return for a touchdown by cornerback Andre Dyson. But afterward, all the talk was about McNair.

"That is one of the best games I have ever seen him play," Titans owner Bud Adams said. "I'd rate it close to the top, if not the top."

GOAL-LINE STAND HELPS TITANS HOLD OFF JAGS
TITANS 10, JAGUARS 3
Date: November 16, 2003
Site: The Coliseum

For six consecutive weeks during the 2003 season, the Titans won games on the strength of their offense. They set a franchise record by scoring at least 30 points in six straight games leading up to a Week 11 contest against the Jaguars at the Coliseum.

And that's when their defense rose to the occasion. The Titans used a turn-back-the-clock goal-line stand to hold off the Jaguars in a 10–3 win, this time bailing out the offense for non-support.

The Titans scored the only touchdown of the game on a five-yard touchdown toss from quarterback Steve McNair to receiver Justin McCareins. Then, leading by a touchdown in the final minutes, the defense had to make it hold up.

Jacksonville was in great position to force overtime, with a first-and-goal at the Tennessee 3-yard line with 2:34 remaining. On first down, Titans linebacker Rocky Calmus and defensive end Juqua Thomas stopped Jaguars running back Chris Fuamatu-Ma'afala for a one-yard loss. On second down, Calmus paired with defensive tackle Rien Long to stop Fuamatu-Ma'afala for a one-yard loss again. The Coliseum crowd was rocking, encouraging the defense even more.

After a delay of game, Jaguars quarterback Byron Leftwich completed a pass to Cortez Hankton, but Titans safety Scott McGarrahan tackled him on the 2-yard line. On fourth down, Leftwich threw an incompletion, and the Titans ran out the clock. Game over.

"It was a gut-check game," defensive tackle Robaire Smith said. "It might not have been real pretty, but we won."

TITANS RALLY TO BEAT FALCONS
TITANS 38, FALCONS 31
Date: November 23, 2003
Site: Georgia Dome, Atlanta

The Titans had plenty of reasons to pack it in early in Atlanta—21 of them to be exact.

When their starting quarterback Steve McNair left the game with a calf injury, it provided yet another. But this team, on this particular day, would have nothing of it. With back-up quarterback Billy Volek guiding the way down the stretch, the Titans rallied from a 21–0 first-quarter deficit to come back and beat the Falcons 38–31 at the Georgia Dome. The comeback was the organization's greatest since the 1979 season.

"This was a character game," coach Jeff Fisher said. "I'm proud of the guys."

After giving up two big plays to Atlanta early, the Titans settled down and began to take over. McNair threw two touchdown passes to tight end Frank Wycheck to cut the deficit to 21–14 before he suffered his injury. McNair wasn't able to return, leaving the rest for Volek, who was up to the challenge.

It was 24–14 Atlanta when the Titans really turned it up, scoring first on a two-yard touchdown run by Eddie George to cut it to 24–21. Less than three minutes later, Justin McCareins returned a punt 59 yards for a touchdown to give the Titans a 28–24 lead.

"It says a lot about us," cornerback Samari Rolle said. "We never quit. And we had some guys step up who had not been asked to do much in the past."

It was the most extensive playing time for Volek up until then, as he had only been used in preseason games and in just a handful of snaps during his first four NFL seasons. In time, he would eventually get more of a chance. Volek completed 9 of 15 passes for 117 yards and a touchdown in the game, and his 14-yard touchdown pass to McCareins in the fourth quarter added the final cushion.

"I don't even know that guy's name," Falcons linebacker Keith Brooking said of Volek. "I don't know where he's from, where he came from. But he played well, that's for sure."

Billy Volek drops back to pass against the Buffalo Bills on December 14, 2003. (Photo by Robert Laberge/Getty Images)

MCNAIR PASS CAPS COMEBACK WIN AT HOUSTON
TITANS 27, TEXANS 24
Date: December 21, 2003
Site: Reliant Stadium, Houston

The crowd at Reliant Stadium was roaring, the Houston Texans in prime position to land their first victory ever over the franchise that left their city not too many years earlier.

After leading nearly the entire game, the Titans were in trouble, down to their final possession and needing a touchdown. Then quarterback Steve McNair calmly led them down the field and broke a lot of hearts in Houston.

On a day when the Titans clinched a playoff berth, they pulled another one out of a hat with a 27–24 victory over the Texans. The game-winning touchdown came on a fourth-and-10 from the Houston 23. That's when McNair dropped back and found receiver Drew Bennett open in the back of the end zone. Moments earlier, the crowd aimed chants of

"overrated" at McNair, who would eventually be named co-MVP of the NFL at the end of the season.

"I don't think the people in the stands realized who was back there at quarterback for us," receiver Derrick Mason said. "They were cheering like they had the game won."

Not too long before, it looked like the Texans did. The Titans led 10–3 at halftime and then 17–10 midway through the third quarter after cornerback Samari Rolle scooped up a fumble and returned it 61 yards for a touchdown. But the Texans wouldn't fold, and with just 1:48 remaining in the game, they ended up taking the lead at 24–20 on a five-yard touchdown run by Domanick Davis.

After getting the kickoff, the Titans began their game-winning drive at their own 25 with 1:42 remaining. After an incompletion, McNair connected with Bennett for 20 yards, then running back Chris Brown picked up eight more. On a second-and-2 from the Houston 47, McNair then connected with Bennett again, this time for 24 yards. Suddenly, the Titans had the ball at the Houston 23 with 37 seconds left.

"Situations like that, that's what you play for," said Bennett. "The crowd was going crazy."

After first spiking the ball to stop the clock, McNair threw two incompletions in the direction of receiver Justin McCareins. Then, faced with the fourth-and-10, and a winner-take-all scenario, McNair chose all. He found Bennett, who shushed the crowd after making the catch. The Titans didn't know they'd have McNair until just a few hours before kickoff—he had missed the previous week's game with a cracked bone spur in his left ankle and hardly practiced all week.

"I just can't talk about him any more," tight end Frank Wycheck said of McNair. "There are no more words to describe what this guy is capable of doing. I've seen it year-in, year-out—game in, game out.... It's just flabbergasting."

TITANS WIN PLAYOFF GAME AT BALTIMORE IN 2003
TITANS 20, RAVENS 17
Date: January 3, 2004
Site: M&T Bank Stadium, Baltimore

Titans running back Eddie George displayed the heart of a champion, refusing to sit out the second half despite dislocating his left shoulder in the second quarter. And the Titans, against their old nemesis from Baltimore, refused to lose in a playoff game that was filled with emotions before, during, and afterward.

When it was all over, it was the Titans celebrating a 20–17 AFC Wild Card Game win over the Ravens, as kicker Gary Anderson's 46-yard field goal barely made it over the crossbar with 23 seconds left, setting off a wild celebration.

"This isn't some fairy tale, some David-and-Goliath thing," Titans tackle Brad Hopkins said. "We knew we had the capabilities to win the game, and we were determined to win it."

Still, few gave the Titans a chance going in. The Ravens had won five straight games in the series, and there was irritating talk that they had Titans' number. As the game played out, the Titans dominated but allowed Baltimore to hang around with mistakes. It seemed eerily similar to their mistake-filled playoff loss to the Ravens that ended their 2000 season.

This night, however, proved to be different. George, among others, helped make sure of that. With McNair struggling—he threw three interceptions in the contest—the

Chris Brown leaps through the hands of a Texans defender during the Titans' 27–24 victory over Houston on December 21, 2003. (Photo by Brian Bahr/Getty Images)

Gary Anderson connects on a 46-yard game-winning field goal as Craig Hentrich holds. The Titans defeated the Baltimore Ravens 20–17 in the AFC Wild Card playoff game on January 3, 2004. (Photo by Doug Pensinger/Getty Images)

Titans relied on George, bum shoulder and all. George dislocated the shoulder making a tackle following a McNair interception in the second quarter. He had it popped back in, and when X-rays showed no damage, he had trainers wrap it in a harness and returned to provide crucial runs.

"Eddie ran over Ray Lewis a couple of times, and that gets the line excited," tackle Fred Miller said.

George showed plenty of emotion while racking up 88 yards on 25 carries. He had one memorable post-play shouting match with Lewis, who, along with his Raven teammates, had been able to boast of past victories against George and the Titans.

"I could have fed into everything that was being said, how they had my number and Ray was in my head," George said. "But I chose to focus on the fact that this was an opportunity to go out and battle for something greater than my personal pride."

At age 44, Anderson put the final dagger in Baltimore's heart. Baltimore led the Titans 10–7 at halftime of the contest, but the Titans took a 14–10 lead on a 49-yard touchdown pass from McNair to receiver Justin McCareins. After a 45-yard field goal by Anderson made it 17–10, the Ravens tied the score at 17–17 when tight end Todd Heap caught a 35-yard touchdown pass from quarterback Anthony Wright.

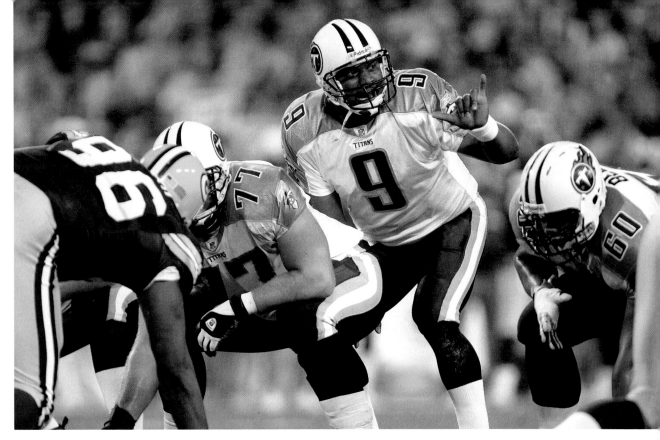

Steve McNair calls a play at the line of scrimmage during the Titans' 48–27 victory over the Green Bay Packers on October 11, 2004. (Photo by Matthew Stockman/Getty Images)

Anderson got into position for the game-winner after the Titans moved the ball from their own 37 to the Baltimore 28 as part of an eight-play drive, with George converting a key third-and-1 with an eight-yard run along the way.

"There was a certain amount of pressure, but I have been in those situations many, many times," Anderson said. "It was exciting."

The following week, the Titans had to deal with heartache in the coldest game in franchise history. In frigid Foxboro, Mass., where the game-time temperature was 4 degrees at kickoff with a wind chill of minus-10, the Titans lost 17–14 to the New England Patriots to end their 2003 season.

BIG DAY AT GREEN BAY ON *MONDAY NIGHT FOOTBALL*
TITANS 48, PACKERS 27
Date: October 11, 2004
Site: Lambeau Field, Green Bay,

For one glorious night in 2004, the Titans looked like one of the NFL's best teams.

They intercepted Green Bay's future Hall of Fame quarterback Brett Favre three times, part of six turnovers they created in a surprising 48–27 win. It was the most points scored by the Titans since 1999.

They scored 17 first-quarter points, matching the Titans' highest point total in any game during the first four weeks of the year. And the 48 points they scored turned out to be the most allowed by the Packers in the history of Lambeau Field and the most scored by a Jeff Fisher-coached team.

"We definitely needed to get our swagger back," safety Tank Williams said. "It was definitely good."

Unfortunately for the Titans, it didn't last in what turned out to be a 5–11 season. But it was sure fun for a night and for Titans fans watching at home on the *Monday Night Football* telecast. It was a shock for many, as the team entered with a record of just 1–3.

The action early was fast and furious. Running back Chris Brown scored on a 37-yard run just 1:29 seconds into the game. Barely four minutes later he was in the end zone again, this time from 29 yards out. It was part of a 148-yard effort by Brown. Quarterback Steve McNair played a mistake-free game, throwing for 206 yards and a pair of touchdowns. Receiver Drew Bennett even added a touchdown throw, a 26-yarder to Derrick Mason.

With as much fun as the guys on offense had, the players on defense seemed to enjoy themselves equally. Safety Lamont Thompson had two interceptions, and Williams had another as the Titans built a 41–13 lead early in the fourth quarter.

"Before the game that was the loosest I have seen everybody this season," cornerback Samari Rolle said. "I knew we were going to come in here and win."

TITANS RALLY TO BEAT GIANTS
TITANS 24, N.Y. GIANTS 21
Date: November 26, 2006
Site: LP Field, Nashville

Fans hugged and cheered in the stands at LP Field, throwing popcorn into the air and their arms around one another. On the field and in the locker room afterward, the celebration scene was pretty much the same among Titans players and coaches.

After pulling off one of the most improbable wins in NFL history—a 24–21 victory over the New York Giants—the Titans and their fans had the feeling that maybe they'd finally gotten over the hump. Looking back, it was perhaps the franchise's biggest turning-point win after two down seasons. The Titans rallied from a 21-point fourth-quarter deficit to get the victory, making everyone want to party like it was 1999.

"The Music City Miracle is really the only time that I've felt like this," said punter Craig Hentrich, referring to the team's playoff win over Buffalo during the 1999 Super Bowl season. "I don't know how you cannot call it a turning-point win. To never lose sight of what we needed to do and to come back like we did, it is something special."

The Titans ended up winning the game on a 49-yard field goal with six seconds remaining by kicker Rob Bironas, capping the biggest fourth-quarter comeback in team history. It was the biggest comeback in the NFL since the 2003 season. It came on a day when perhaps a legend was born in Tennessee in rookie quarterback Vince Young, who engineered the comeback.

"Rookies aren't supposed to do stuff like that, but that's Vince. I have been trying to tell you guys," said tight end Bo Scaife, who was also Young's teammate at the University of Texas. "I remember when we were down 35–0 vs. Oklahoma State my senior year and he led us back to beat them. Vince is not a quitter, and nobody on this team is either."

Young, who threw for 249 yards in the game and ran for 69 more, led the biggest comeback in NFL history by a rookie quarterback. Hall of Famer John Elway held the record previously when he guided the Broncos back from a 19–0 deficit to beat the Colts 21–19 in 1983.

Many of the fans missed the comeback, leaving after the Titans fell down 21–0 after three quarters. Tennessee's comeback started when cornerback Pacman Jones picked off an

Rob Bironas kicks the winning field goal in the final seconds of the Titans' 24–21 victory over the New York Giants on November 26, 2006. (Photo by Tim Umphrey/Getty Images)

Eli Manning pass at the New York 46 with 12:55 remaining in the game. Just over three minutes later, the Titans made it 21–7 when Young completed a four-yard touchdown pass to Scaife.

After holding the Giants, the Titans got the ball back and scored again following a nifty return by Jones, and in just over two minutes they got in the end zone on Young's one-yard run. With 5:24 remaining, suddenly it was 21–14.

"You could feel the energy," fullback Ahmard Hall said. "We believed."

When the Titans stopped the Giants again, forcing a punt, finally they were in control of their own destiny. Young drove the Titans 76 yards in eight plays, converting a fourth-and-10 when he escaped the grasp of Giants defensive end Mathias Kiwanuka. The Titans tied it at 21-all when Young found receiver Brandon Jones open for a 14-yard touchdown pass with 44 seconds remaining.

Another interception by Pacman Jones set up Bironas' game-winning kick.

"It's a sneak peek of what's going to happen, not just with me, but with this team in general," Young said. "It's a sneak peek of how our future can be if we just continue to play hard and keep working to get to the point we want to be."

"When the light switch finally came on for us, everything changed," Brandon Jones said. "Guys kept saying, 'This game ain't over. It's not over.' ...This is one of the greatest wins I've ever been a part of."

For the Giants, it was more than a heartbreaker. They dominated for three quarters, getting two touchdown runs from Brandon Jacobs and a three-yard touchdown pass from Manning to receiver Plaxico Burress to build the big lead.

"It's [a] terrible shock to everybody in the organization, for everybody. There's no excuse; there's no nothing," Giants coach Tom Coughlin said. "We had that ball game well in hand and we didn't finish the game.... We're going to be sick about this one forever."

BIRONAS' 60-YARD FIELD GOAL BEATS COLTS
TITANS 20, COLTS 17
Date: December 3, 2006
Site: LP Field

As the football flew through air, time stood still for a few moments at LP Field. Titans kicker Rob Bironas watched, hoping and praying his 60-yard attempt had enough. On the sideline, coach Jeff Fisher was doing the same, as were the other Titans surrounding him.

"I was probably one of the only ones who didn't look at it," safety Chris Hope said. "I just wanted to let the crowd tell me what happened."

Hope got the response he was looking for—and so did the Titans. Bironas' 60-yard field goal with just seven seconds left lifted the Titans to a 20–17 victory over the Indianapolis Colts, the team's second dramatic win in as many weeks. It gave the Titans their third straight win in 2006, the longest streak since the '03 season. Most of the fans on hand at chilly LP Field had a hard time believing what they had just seen long after it was over. The Titans rallied from a two-touchdown deficit against the Colts, who would go on to win Super Bowl XLI. Bironas' kick was the longest in franchise history, and it was just three yards shy of the NFL record.

"All you have to do is get baby sharks to taste blood and they will sink their teeth in," Titans linebacker Keith Bulluck said afterward. "We are a young team and a lot of guys

Brandon Jones hauls in a touchdown pass during the second half of the Titans' 20–17 victory over the Indianapolis Colts on December 3, 2006. (Photo by G. Newman Lowrance/NFL/Getty Images)

don't know what it takes to win in this league—or they didn't know what it takes. Guys are finding out. Now it's getting to the point where we're expecting to win games like this."

After the game, many Titans stayed on the field to celebrate with their ecstatic fans. Players like Drew Bennett, Ahmard Hall, and Bobby Wade made a victory lap, slapping hands with those in the front row. Moments earlier, they all watched the Titans pull off another improbable upset.

An hour after the game, Bironas stood on the Titans logo at midfield, posing with family members from the spot his game-winning kick took flight, with a nice wind behind it.

"The Titans win, and that is what the bottom line is," Bironas said.

In other ways, it was more than that. "I just get tired of people talking (bad) about us," Titans quarterback Vince Young said. "When you have people saying we are the worst team in the league you get tired of hearing that, especially when you know you are a good team.… Everyone is working together and continues to believe and fights until there is no time on the clock."

Colts quarterback Peyton Manning threw for 351 yards in the game, but the Colts were held to just three points in the second half. The Colts were aiming to clinch the AFC South title, but it didn't happen.

The Titans fell behind 14–0 early but rallied behind Young. The Titans took the lead 17–14 in the third quarter when Young connected with receiver Brandon Jones for a nine-yard touchdown pass. After the Colts tied it at 17-all with 2:38 remaining on a 20-yard field goal by kicker Adam Vinatieri—following a defensive stop by the Titans near the goal line—Young worked his magic again.

In nine plays, Young drove the Titans to the Indianapolis 42-yard line with 12 seconds left, completing an 18-yard pass to Bobby Wade along the way. Then the Titans left it to Bironas.

"It is hard to find a team this late in the season with little chance of making the playoffs to come out and compete as hard as we do, and that is what we're doing every week," Hope said. "At this point in the season you'll find guys worrying about shipping their cars back home, guys with children, trying to get them back in school in hometowns, focusing on everything but football. But this team has continued to work and keep a positive attitude. And we're finding ways to win games."

YOUNG RUNS FOR OT SCORE IN HOUSTON HOMECOMING

TITANS 26, TEXANS 20 (OT)
Date: December 10, 2006
Site: Reliant Stadium, Houston

All the buzz leading up to the game was about Vince Young's homecoming. After all, in the eyes of plenty of Houstonians, the Titans quarterback should have been a Texan.

On Young's return trip to his hometown, the rookie quarterback made them pay with some late-game heroics. He ran 39 yards for the game-winning touchdown in overtime, lifting the Titans to a 26–20 win over the Texans. It was the team's fourth straight victory and the third straight in dramatic fashion. The Texans ended up being the goats, one for their decision to blitz the elusive Young on the deciding play and, in the eyes of many in the state, for passing on the former University of Texas star in the NFL Draft.

"You couldn't have written a better script for Vince, to come back home and win like that," Titans guard Jacob Bell said. "It was a storybook finish for him, like a movie script. A perfect ending, both for him and the team."

The Texans could hardly believe their eyes as the Titans swept them for the second year in a row. "It was one of the worst feelings you could possibly have," defensive end Antwan Peek said. "It was an absolute nightmare."

The eyes of Texas were on Young as the Titans got the ball at the start of overtime. At the end of regulation, he had led the team to a go-ahead touchdown, only to see the Texans tie the game on a late field goal. Facing a third-and-14 at the Houston 39 in overtime, the Texans decided to send extra players after Young, instead of dropping back into coverage, which is what they did most the day. When Young noticed that, he stepped up in the pocket and took off downfield, picking up a few key blocks along the way.

"I felt like my mom was chasing me with a belt," Young said of the run. "I saw the lane and used my God-given talents to make things happen."

When he finally crossed the goal line, the Titans were winners again. The victory improved their record to 6-7 on the season. "I've never heard of a walk-off touchdown," linebacker Keith Bulluck said. "But that is what happened."

Running back Travis Henry aided Vince Young's return to Houston with 88 yards rushing in the Titans' 26–20 overtime victory over the Texans on December 10, 2006. (Photo by Stephen Dunn/ Getty Images)

For Young, who played high school football in Houston, the game-winning run capped an emotional week. He immediately threw the football into the stands and blew kisses at the fans, many of them cheering him on in his jerseys, old and new. He pointed to the sky before being swarmed by teammates. Just like he did with the Texans' defense on his final run, Young weaved through cameramen and reporters as he left the field following an interview. A good deal of the crowd stuck around to give him another round of applause.

"It was a great ending, being from Houston and being in front of my family and the fans out there," Young said. "It doesn't get much better than that."

Titans coach Jeff Fisher said he was just hoping to get into field-goal range on the final play, and the Titans had a pass play designed to get it. Kicker Rob Bironas was on the sideline, readying for his third game-winning kick in three weeks. He never got the chance, of course.

"I never want to give Vince Young his props or the recognition he deserves, but he made me a believer on that last play," Texans defensive end N.D. Kalu said. "I didn't know if I wanted to throw my helmet or cry."

The Titans fought back after trailing 14–6 in the third quarter and 17–13 in the fourth.

Young completed 19 of 29 passes for 218 yards and a touchdown in the game and ran for 86 more yards, including the game-winner. Running back Travis Henry ran for 88 yards and two touchdowns on 20 carries.

DEFENSE SCORES THREE TDS
IN WILD WIN OVER JAGS
TITANS 24, JAGUARS 17
Date: December 17, 2006
Site: LP Field, Nashville

Titans linebacker Keith Bulluck issued his defensive teammates a challenge before they took the field against the Jacksonville Jaguars. He told them stopping the Jaguars wasn't going to be enough that day. He wanted defensive touchdowns, too. Obviously, they took the pep talk to heart.

The Titans' defense posted a hat trick in the team's 24–17 over the Jaguars by scoring three defensive touchdowns for the first time in the franchise's 47-year history. It was the team's fifth straight win. "Play-making becomes contagious, just like winning does," said safety Chris Hope, who had one of the defensive scores. "Once you get on a roll, everybody wants to be a part of the celebration, or the win."

The win was payback for the Jaguars, who pounded the Titans 37–7 the previous month and had won the past two meetings by a combined score of 77–20. "They had a swagger coming in like we weren't nothing," said cornerback Reynaldo Hill, whose interception with 38 seconds left clinched it. "I saw those guys talking about us this week, saying, 'It's just the Titans, we'll be fine.' That was a punch in the face to us. That's no respect for us. I think they believe we're for real now. Some of their guys even told me."

In previous weeks, the Titans made a habit of winning on offense, but this was a day reserved for the defense. The Titans returned turnovers 83, 92, and 61 yards for touchdowns, and that was part of a franchise-record three defensive TDs and a team-record 370 yards of returns. They won the game despite being out-gained 396–98 in total yardage and despite the fact the Jaguars had 23 first downs to their five.

Cortland Finnegan returns a fumble by Jacksonville quarterback David Garrard 92 yards for a touchdown in the third quarter of the Titans' 24–17 victory over the Jaguars on December 17, 2006. (Photo by Brian Bahr/Getty Images)

Titans defensive back Reynaldo Hill intercepts a pass intended for Buffalo's Josh Reed during the Titans' 30–29 victory over the Bills on December 24, 2006. (Photo by Rick Stewart/Getty Images)

The Jaguars had the ball 44 minutes, 22 seconds compared to 15 minutes, 38 seconds for the Titans. The Jaguars ran 82 plays, compared to just 34 for the Titans. "Crazy?" Titans defensive tackle Albert Haynesworth said. "A win is a win. You can put it in the crazy win column or the close win column or whatever you want to do. As long as we keep winning, that is what I am happy about."

The Jaguars left shaking their heads. In the first quarter, Titans cornerback Pacman Jones intercepted a David Garrard pass and returned it 83 yards for a touchdown. In the third quarter, with the game tied at 10–10, Garrard fumbled, and Titans cornerback Cortland Finnegan picked up the ball and raced 92 yards for a score. Hope completed the scoring with a 61-yard interception return for a touchdown late in the third, which made it 24–10.

"I have never been a part of a day quite like this," Garrard said. "I don't even know if I have seen a day quite like this."

Titans quarterback Vince Young, a hero the previous three weeks, was pretty much a spectator. He threw for just 85 yards and ran for just four more. But he didn't seem to mind.

"Defense, defense, defense," Young said. "They made plays. It goes to show that it doesn't just take offense to win games. It takes offense, defense, special teams to win the game. Overall, the defense had the upper hand today. I applaud those guys a whole lot."

TITANS RALLY TO WIN IN BUFFALO
TITANS 30, BILLS 29
Date: December 24, 2006
Site: Ralph Wilson Stadium, Orchard Park, N.Y.

On Christmas Eve, the Titans continued to create magic. They managed to find yet another way to win a football game, their sixth in a row, this time rallying to beat the Buffalo Bills. They won this one 30–29 on kicker Rob Bironas' 30-yard field goal with just 2:10 remaining.

"It shows a lot about how resilient we are," linebacker Keith Bulluck said. "We've been in just about every situation this year. We've been down a lot and we've come back and won. We've won when we haven't played especially well. But we know there is always a way for us to win."

With winds swirling and their playoff hopes flickering, the Titans were down 29–20 at the start of the fourth quarter. But just like they'd done in previous weeks, they rallied, first getting a 29-yard touchdown pass from quarterback Vince Young to receiver Brandon Jones with 11:14 remaining to cut the lead to 29–27. That set the stage for Bironas' game-winning kick.

"I don't know if we are a team of destiny, but we have something special going on around here," Jones said. "We are a team, and winning as one."

The game featured seven lead changes, but the Titans held it last when Bironas' kick capped a 14-play, 75-yard drive that started at the Tennessee 12-yard line with 9:25 left. Young converted two third-down plays on the drive—one with his arm, the other with his legs—to put the Titans in position for the kick.

Buffalo had a chance to win it late, driving to the Tennessee 28-yard line in the final minute. But Titans cornerback Reynaldo Hill intercepted a J.P. Losman pass to seal the win.

"I'm always happy to win," Young said. "Whatever it takes from an offense, defense, and special teams standpoint. We had some ups and downs in the game and the win was real crazy out there, but we got the 'W' and that's all that matters."

Despite the tough conditions, Young threw for 183 yards and two touchdowns and also had 61 yards on the ground, including a 36-yard touchdown run with one second remaining in the first half when he weaved through the Buffalo defense.

Running back Travis Henry also played a key role in beating his old team. Henry carried the ball 25 times for 135 yards and had some key plays on the team's game-winning drive. In the game, he also went over the 1,000-yard mark for the season. Jones had 101 receiving yards and the important touchdown.

"This is one of the games I had circled on my calendar when I found out we were playing (the Bills)," Henry said. "It was a big game for me and with my teammates behind me.... We had a lot of fun out there."

After an 0–5 start, the win in Buffalo raised the team's record to 8–7. But the Titans ended up losing to the Patriots, 40–23, the next week and were eliminated from the playoffs.

SEASON-OPENING WIN OVER JAGS IN 2007

TITANS 13, JAGUARS 10
Date: September 9, 2007
Site: Jacksonville Municipal Stadium, Jacksonville

On the NFL's opening weekend, the Titans were big underdogs playing in a hostile environment. But they played the role of the bully against the Jaguars, pushing them around in a 13–10 win that made quite an opening impression. They did it with a record-setting rushing attack and physical, run-stopping defense.

"I think a lot of people are probably shocked by this," Titans defensive tackle Albert Haynesworth said. "People on the outside probably think we are just some mediocre team that's probably at the bottom of the league.

"But it is going to be different this year. It's a different team, and I think we showed some of that."

It was clearly a far cry from the start of the previous season, when the Titans started 0–5 and finished one game short of making the playoffs. "I heard a lot of the players say 'We're back,'" coach Jeff Fisher said. "Well, we've only won one game. So we're not necessarily back yet. But at least we can carry some confidence into Week 2."

With running back Chris Brown leading the way with a career-high 175 yards, the Titans piled up 282 yards on the ground as a team. That total was second only to the franchise record of 296 yards set in a 1997 game against the Chiefs. Making it more impressive is the fact it came against a Jacksonville team that finished the previous year ranked fourth in run defense, allowing just 91.3 yards per game. It was the most rushing yards ever allowed by a Jaguar team.

"They knew what we were running a lot of times and they still couldn't stop it," said Brown, who ran for just 156 yards total the previous year.

The Titans also stopped the run, holding the Jaguars to only 72 rushing yards. The Jaguars averaged twice that many yards on the ground with the same two backs—Maurice Jones-Drew and Fred Taylor—the previous year. For the Titans, it was a sign of things to come the rest of the year.

"We weren't a good run defense last year and today we were a very good run defense," defensive end Kyle Vanden Bosch said. "It looks like we've fixed some things."

The Titans trailed 10–6 at halftime but took the lead for good on a two-yard touchdown run by Young, who completed 11 of 18 passes for 78 yards in the contest. Running back LenDale White added 66 yards on 18 carries for the Titans.

TITANS SHINE IN PRIME TIME AT NEW ORLEANS

TITANS 31, SAINTS 14
Date: September 24, 2007
Site: The Superdome, New Orleans

The rest of America got a chance to see what many in Nashville were starting to believe— the Titans had a playoff-caliber team. In their first *Monday Night Football* appearance since the 2004 season, the Titans went to the Superdome and pushed the New Orleans Saints around, winning 31–14.

Quarterback Vince Young directed several key scoring drives, playing one of his best games of the season. And linebacker Keith Bulluck lived up to his "Mr. Monday Night"

LenDale White looks for running room in the Titans' 13–10 victory over the Jacksonville Jaguars on September 9, 2007. (Photo by Doug Benc/Getty Images)

nickname, intercepting three passes. It lifted the Titans to 2–1, their best start since the 2003 season.

"The secret is out of the bag now," center Kevin Mawae said. "We are a lot better than probably a lot of people thought we would be."

It was the Titans' fifth straight road game, dating back to the '06 season, which tied a franchise record for consecutive road games.

"We are just going to keep playing football and hopefully teams will start to take us seriously," Bulluck said. "I have been on great teams with great players and we still didn't get fair justice. But that's OK. We'll just keeping playing and just let it play out."

The Titans jumped out to a 10–0 lead early, scoring on a 35-yard touchdown strike from Young to receiver Brandon Jones. Young was 14-for-22 for 164 yards and two touchdowns on the night.

After the Saints rallied to take a 14–10 lead on a pair of one-yard touchdown runs by running back Reggie Bush, the Titans got off the mat. They reclaimed the lead at 17–14 on a one-yard run by LenDale White, and early in the fourth quarter Young connected with tight end Bo Scaife for a three-yard touchdown. The Titans clinched it on a 61-yard interception return by safety Vincent Fuller late in the fourth quarter. After the game, Young was so excited he threw his wristbands into the crowd, then took off his shoes and tossed then into the crowd as souvenirs as well.

"Everyone was worried about their offense and what they were doing, but they needed to worry about us," Scaife said. "We wanted to go in there, play hard, and show the rest of the NFL we're for real."

BIRONAS MAKES EIGHT FIELD GOALS
TITANS 38, TEXANS 36
Date: October 21, 2007
Site: Reliant Stadium, Houston

Fans came wanting to see Vince Young. Instead, they got a whole lot of Titans kicker Rob Bironas, who set an NFL record with eight field goals, and a gutsy performance from back-up quarterback Kerry Collins, who guided the Titans to a late scoring drive. Combined, they helped save the Titans from an embarrassing collapse.

"Have you ever seen anything like that?" Collins asked after the Titans' 38–36 win over the Texans in Houston. "I'd have to say that is probably the craziest game I have ever been involved in."

Collins ran off the field at Reliant Stadium to chants of "Kerry, Kerry, Kerry," which came from a small pocket of Titans fans. The majority of those in the crowd were crushed after watching the home team rally from a 32–7 fourth-quarter deficit to take the lead with 57 seconds left, only to lose. A last-minute drive engineered by Collins, filling in for an injured Young, put the Titans in position for a 29-yard field goal by Bironas, which won the game on the final play and set an NFL record in the process.

In winning, the Titans improved to 4–2. Young watched from the sideline with a strained quad, one season after some late-game heroics of his own in the same stadium.

"Hey, we won," center Kevin Mawae said. "Yeah, we had opportunities to put the game out of reach and we didn't. And that is the frustrating part. But we are not walking out this door backwards and ashamed of what happened."

Tight end Bo Scaife celebrates his touchdown during the Titans' 31–14 victory over the New Orleans Saints on September 24, 2007. (Photo by Chris Graythen/Getty Images)

Running back Chris Brown crosses into the end zone for a touchdown against the Houston Texans on December 2, 2007. (Photo by Chris McGrath/Getty Images)

Collins completed 25 of 42 passes for 280 yards, guiding the Titans to their biggest point total since the 2004 season. With the game on the line, he came through. After the Titans fell behind 36–35 on a 53-yard pass from quarterback Sage Rosenfels to Andre Davis with 57 seconds left, Collins drove the Titans 69 yards to the Houston 17-yard line in just six plays, setting up Bironas for the game-winner. The key play was a 46-yard completion to receiver Roydell Williams on the sideline.

"All of a sudden we went from a position to where we were trying to chew time off the clock to 'Hey, we have to go win this game,'" Collins said. "That's part of life in the NFL, you have to be able to refocus under some wild circumstances and that's what we did."

On the day, Bironas was a perfect eight for eight. The eight field goals broke an NFL record for kicks in a game. Later in the week, the Pro Football Hall of Fame in Canton, Ohio, would be shipped the football from the record-breaking kick, and at the end of the '07 season it received Bironas' right cleat as well.

"The offense kept putting me into position to kick field goals," Bironas said. "I just went out there and did my job."

5

GENERATION NEXT

by Bob McClellan

Of the players ranked among the top 10 Titans of the franchise's first 10 years in Nashville, five are active in the NFL. Three—Keith Bulluck, Craig Hentrich, and Jevon Kearse—still play for the Titans.

Bulluck is the youngest of the three and 2008 will mark his ninth season in the league. It's safe to say in another 10 years, when the Titans are celebrating their 20th anniversary, none of them will be active. Who are the superstars of tomorrow for the Titans? Which players have a chance to crack the top 10 or extend the list to 20 over the course of the next decade?

Coach Jeff Fisher and general manager Mike Reinfeldt hope they are building toward another run like the one from 1999-2003 that produced a 56–24 regular-season record, five playoff victories and a Super Bowl appearance. There are some similarities between the 1999 team and the 2008 team. The 1999 team was led by a dual-threat quarterback and former first-round pick who was just coming into his

The Titans began their next generation the same way they began the last one: with a dual-threat quarterback. This time, it's Vince Young's turn. (Photo courtesy Tennessee Titans)

own in fifth-year pro Steve McNair. The '08 team has a dual-threat quarterback and former first-round pick in Vince Young, who while coming under fire for sub-par passing numbers in 2007, is entering only his third year in the NFL.

The 1999 team was powered by the running of Eddie George. The Titans have continued to rush the ball well—it is a Fisher trademark—but the 2008 team doesn't have a hammer the equal of the former Heisman Trophy winner. It does hope to have a home-run threat that the AFC championship team didn't have in rookie running back Chris Johnson. The 5'11", 195-pounder out of East Carolina was the fastest player at the NFL Combine, covering the 40-yard dash in a jaw-dropping 4.24 seconds.

The leading receiver for the 1999 Titans was tight end Frank Wycheck. Could Young develop the same chemistry with free-agent tight end Alge Crumpler? The former Atlanta Falcon is a four-time Pro Bowl selection who has caught at least five touchdown passes in each of the last four seasons. Given Young's propensity to throw to the tight end, the 6'2", 262-pound Crumpler is a big target who could put up big numbers.

The defense of the 1999 team could really get after the passer. In fact, it set a then-franchise record with 54 sacks, led by Kearse's 14.5. The 2008 Titans could be a 50-plus sack team with the return of Kearse and the play up front of 2007 Pro Bowlers Albert Haynesworth and Kyle Vanden Bosch.

The secondary on the 1999 team also was a solid unit. It mixed a couple of younger players (cornerbacks Samari Rolle and Denard Walker) with a couple of veterans (safeties Blaine Bishop and Marcus Robertson). The 2008 team features upstarts Cortland Finnegan, a third-year corner, and Michael Griffin, a second-year safety who was the Titans' first pick in the 2007 draft, along with veterans Chris Hope at strong safety and cornerback Nick Harper.

And let us not forget the special teams. Hentrich, like Kearse, is a holdover from the 1999 team. He also will handle the punting duties in 2008. The placekicker on the current team is Rob Bironas, who comes off his first Pro Bowl appearance. He made 35 of 39 field goal attempts in 2007, including an NFL-record eight field goals against the Houston Texans on Oct. 21.

So which players have the best chance of being a part of "Generation Next?" Here's a look at three of the top candidates:

VINCE YOUNG

If not for Vince Young's performance against USC in the Rose Bowl at the conclusion of the 2005 season, who knows if he would be a Titan today? What he did against the Trojans not only will live in college football lore forever, but also moved him front and center into the debate of not only who should be the first quarterback taken in the 2006 draft, but who should be the No. 1 overall selection.

Young carved up the favored Trojans in the national title game. On a field full of future NFL players, he was quite simply better than all of them. He completed 30 of 40 passes for 267 yards with no interceptions, and he rushed for 200 yards and three touchdowns on 19 carries. Two of his touchdowns came in the final 4 minutes, 3 seconds, including the game-winner on a fourth down from the USC 8-yard line with 19 seconds to play. Texas prevailed 41–38, and Young was named MVP.

"We didn't understand how big and strong the guy really is," USC defensive end Frostee Rucker said. "When you see a guy standing eye-to-eye to you, and he weighs just as much as you weigh, he poses a threat."

Vince Young tucks the ball and takes off for a run against the New England Patriots. (Photo courtesy Tennessee Titans)

He does indeed. The Rose Bowl victory was a tantalizing showing of athleticism and daring, reminiscent of the early years of McNair as a Titan. The franchise was intrigued enough to make Young the third overall pick and first quarterback taken, ahead of Matt Leinart and Jay Cutler. It agreed to pay him $58 million over five years with an option for a sixth year, and his signing bonus was almost $26 million.

"One of the highlights of my career was having a 10-year run more or less with Steve McNair, now I'm looking forward to another 10-year run with Vince," Fisher said. "(Offensive coordinator) Mike Heimerdinger got Steve in his fourth year as a starter and two years later he was the co-MVP. We're fortunate to get Mike back in here and he gets Vince as a third-year starter."

Fisher had a notion to bring Young along slowly, just as he had McNair. But veteran Kerry Collins struggled to pick up the offense in his first season as the starter, and when the Titans stumbled to an 0–3 start, the job quickly belonged to the rookie. At Texas, Young was

30–2 as a starter. He certainly didn't feel like his taking the reins should be viewed as the team giving up and throwing him into the fire.

"If you think like that, it will be like that," Young said. "But if you have confidence that this rookie guy is going to come in and make plays like Matt Leinart or Jay Cutler or any of those guys, if you believe in those guys, you can win."

The Titans didn't immediately win with Young under center either. In fact, they went 0–2 in his first couple of starts, and it didn't sit well with him. After all, it took three years and 32 games for him to amass two losses at Texas.

"We've just got to believe in each other more," Young said after his first start. "I believe we've got to have more fun. I mean, I love this game so much it's ridiculous. I love it just as [much as] I love my mom. That's how I've got to get these guys to feel, like that. I've got to let these guys know, 'Hey, man, let's go, even though we're down.' That's when our competitiveness is supposed to come out."

The Titans stood at 0–5. They could have packed it in for the season. NFL pundits expected it. No one would have been surprised. Instead, Young renewed the Titans' faith in him, and Fisher coaxed his team to a remarkable turnaround. Tennessee won eight of its final 11 games and nearly sneaked into the playoffs. Meanwhile, the new QB ran off to win the Associated Press Offensive Rookie of the Year Award.

Young was everything the team dreamed he could be over the final 11 games, engineering fourth-quarter comebacks, taking off on improbable scrambles, zipping the ball all over the field. By the time all was said and done he had passed for 2,199 yards and 12 touchdowns and rushed for 552 yards and seven scores.

The rushing totals were staggering. He averaged 6.7 yards per carry. No rookie QB in the Super Bowl era had surpassed 500 yards on the ground. He also became the first rookie in league history to have three touchdown passes of 20 yards or longer and three touchdown runs of 20 yards or longer. He became only the third quarterback to win the award in its 30-year history.

> " *I love this game so much it's ridiculous. I love it just as [much as] I love my mom.* "

"Each week my teammates talked about it and then my family members said, 'You might win Rookie of the Year,'" Young said. "It was always one of my goals. I wanted to do something each week to give them an eye to look at me for Rookie of the Year because my teammates did an awesome job of getting me motivated, getting me pumped up and then also having my back out there."

Fisher was pleased with Young's development during his first season, but the coach also made sure the spotlight was shared.

"I think the thing that is interesting to point out, and is important to point out, is that I only see a couple of other quarterbacks on this list, and that's hard. That's hard to do. The position is such—and even more so now than in the past—a difficult position to play early in your career," Fisher said. "To get the recognition that he got, we think is terrific. Credit goes to his teammates because without the offensive line, the running backs, the receivers on the other end of the throws, the defense and the field position, the special teams things, none of this would have been possible."

Young's fantastic first season wasn't over yet. When Phillip Rivers pulled out of the Pro Bowl due to injury, Young was added to the AFC roster. He was the first rookie quarterback invited to Hawaii since Dan Marino in 1983.

"It was a great week, a great experience," Young said. "I had a good time with my family, a good time with the players. Playing in this game with all these guys—it doesn't get any better than that."

All of the accolades raised expectations for Young's second season, perhaps to outsized proportions. While the Titans managed to go 10–6 and make the playoffs, Young had just nine touchdown passes and 17 interceptions. He rushed for 395 yards and three touchdowns. At least his completion percentage was up significantly from his rookie season, from 51.5 percent to 62.3 percent.

In his playoff debut, Young completed 16 of 29 passes for 138 yards and an interception as the visiting Titans fell 17–6 to the San Diego Chargers. "For my first time in the playoffs, I really feel like I did all right," Young said. "I could have done a little bit better, but at the same time I just played the game and took what the defense gave me. Just talking to my coaches, they said I was very poised and I played pretty good. I just need to finish."

Young wasn't always satisfied with his play during the 2007 season, but his team still won. Ultimately quarterbacks are measured on winning. You won't find former Pittsburgh Steelers quarterback Terry Bradshaw near the top of the all-time list in any statistical category, but you will find him atop the list of Super Bowl-winning QBs (tied with Joe Montana). That also means there is another convenient place to find him…in the Pro Football Hall of Fame.

"We're winning games. That's the bottom line. We're winning games," Fisher said. "He is contributing an awful lot to those wins. If people want 400 or 500 yards passing out of our offense, they're going to have to wait. They're not going to get it. We're not there yet. Whether we ever get there, I don't know. But we're winning games. There are other ways to win games."

Titans linebacker Keith Bulluck, one of the team's leaders, believes Young merely needs to learn more of the nuances of his position. Once the knowledge that comes only with experience kicks in, the veteran won't have any worries about the offense.

"He's just completed his second year. The third and fourth year is when you take that major leap," Bulluck said. "He definitely knows he has to get better and he wants to get better. He wants to be one of the best. He's trying to make himself better and get others around him to work and get better.

"He's got leadership down. But he has to do some fine-tuning at the position. It's the hardest position on the field. It takes time. He's getting his work on the fly. Steve had time to watch for two years. Vince was thrown into the fire and forced to perform. Hopefully he keeps getting better and better. He gets the most out of his players, the guys who play with him. He makes people around him better."

Fisher has continued to defend Young against criticism. "Vince has improved daily, weekly, yearly, and will continue to improve," the coach said. "He's gonna win a lot of games. He's very competitive, has great leadership qualities. He's a very, very talented athlete who's becoming a very good quarterback. He just needs to keep playing. We need to surround him with good people, and keep running the football. It's just experience.

"At some point you experience it all. You get to a point where you can anticipate the third-and-7 throw, the route concept that will allow you to keep a drive alive to win a ballgame. He'll know the middle of this year what we're gonna call on fourth-and-goal from the 9 to win the game. And he'll know where the ball is gonna go. It's experience. You can't accelerate it. It has to happen, and it has been. You can see the results already. It especially takes longer in this day and age for quarterbacks. He'll get there."

KYLE VANDEN BOSCH

Kyle Vanden Bosch was a second-round pick of the Arizona Cardinals in the 2001 draft, but his career didn't heat up in the desert. In fact it almost withered and died.

The former University of Nebraska standout was mostly a bust for the Cards. Injuries wrecked his four years in Arizona. He played in only three games as a rookie before being sidelined for the rest of the season with a torn ACL in his right knee. He came back to start all 16 games in his second season and looked like he might be on his way, but he suffered a torn ACL in his left knee in the 2003 preseason and missed the entire year. He made it back to the field in 2004, but he was tentative and admittedly a shell of his former self. He made one start and had only 15 tackles.

When his contract was up, the Cardinals weren't waiting to re-sign him. He could hardly blame them. "They gave me a chance," Vanden Bosch said. "When I watch tape on myself [in 2004] I wasn't the player I am now. So I don't blame them for anything. I had no sacks and [15] tackles. That's not a guy you want to build your team around. But I knew I was on my way back, I just wasn't there yet."

Would anyone else realize he was on his way back? He didn't figure on the phone ringing off the hook with teams in a bidding war to sign him. "This league isn't really known for giving guys second chances and waiting around for guys to get healthy," Vanden Bosch said. "But I wasn't going to quit. That is not who I am."

The Titans had been intrigued by Vanden Bosch while he was in college, so they inquired when he became a free agent. They brought him to Nashville for a physical, and they liked him enough to sign him to a one-year deal for the veteran minimum of $540,000. It turned out to be a great investment. Vanden Bosch had 6.5 sacks in his first six games in a Titans uniform, and his motor hasn't stopped running since.

"He has been blessed with a unique sense of endurance," Fisher said. "He just goes. I've seen only one motor like his and that was (five-time Pro Bowler) Kevin Greene."

Vanden Bosch is 6'4" and 278 pounds, and with his shaved head and goatee, not to mention his intensity, he certainly can make an impression. "I remember the first time I saw him I was like, 'Who the hell is this guy?'" Titans linebacker Keith Bulluck said. "He had a very serious attitude. He was in the weight room not really talking to anybody. The first time we were on the field he was going 110 mph every single play. That will get people's attention fast. Then when we put the pads on and he's going 110 mph…and he'll hit your ass, too."

Bulluck was thrilled about Vanden Bosch's arrival. Bulluck had been drafted by the Titans in 2000, when they were in the midst of winning 56 regular-season games in a five-year span. He then endured the 2004 season in which they went 5–11 and watched the salary cap force the dismantling of a once-dominant team. In the 2005 season, the Titans bottomed out at 4–12, but at least Bulluck could point to some help on the defensive side.

"He's a great teammate. He's one of those guys we brought in when we were rebuilding who actually helped," Bulluck said. "Kyle's story has been one of my favorites,

Kyle Vanden Bosch has turned out to be one of the best free-agent signings in Titans history. He has already made two Pro Bowl appearances as a Titan. (Photo by Tom Hauck/Getty Images)

to see how he has come in from being nearly out of the NFL to being a two-time Pro Bowler. He's doing a lot of great things for this team and this community. Guys watch him play, watch his approach to practice, the weight room, to everything, and you can't help but to respect it."

> **Kyle's story has been one of my favorites, to see how he has come in from being nearly out of the NFL to being a two-time Pro Bowler.... You can't help but to respect it.**

The coaches moved Vanden Bosch from left defensive end to right defensive end in 2007 so he could line up next to tackle Albert Haynesworth. He responded with 12 sacks and four forced fumbles and his second Pro Bowl as a Titan.

"He especially benefited from switching from left to right to line up next to Albert," Fisher said. "The two of them worked well together. And he benefits from his effort. Kyle is gonna do what Kyle does, Albert helps him, but Kyle still will be productive with or without Albert."

ALBERT HAYNESWORTH

The 2007 version of Albert Haynesworth was the player Titans coaches and fans had been dreaming he would be since he was drafted by the team out of the University of Tennessee in the first round in 2002.

Defensive lineman Albert Haynesworth lines up against the Green Bay Packers at Lambeau Field on September 1, 2006 in Green Bay, Wisconsin. The Titans beat the Packers 35–21. (Photo by David Stluka/Getty Images)

The 6'6", 320-pounder was virtually unstoppable, ripping holes in opposing offensive lines as though he were a battering ram. He had 40 tackles and a career-high eight sacks, and he made his first Pro Bowl.

"I just wanted to go out and show what I could do, show the Titans what they drafted me for and continue doing it all season," Haynesworth said. "I think every year I've been in the NFL I've gotten better. I think this year really showed that and hopefully next year will be even better."

Haynesworth missed three games in November because of injuries, and not coincidentally the Titans lost all three. Actually, they didn't just lose them. They were gouged, yielding an average of 32.3 points and 160 rushing yards per game. Those numbers were in stark contrast to the 13 games in which Haynesworth played. In those games the Titans went 10–3 and gave up only 15.4 points and 76.8 rushing yards.

The difference in the numbers is staggering. Haynesworth was that good in 2007. If he had been able to play all 16 games, he would have been in any discussion for the league's defensive MVP. "He's a real presence, a very disruptive force," Indianapolis Colts quarterback Peyton Manning said.

He and Kyle Vanden Bosch helped each other to Hawaii, with 2007 marking Vanden Bosch's second Pro Bowl appearance. "When he's been healthy he's just been a force," Vanden Bosch said. "Teams have had to game plan around him. He really dictates not only which running plays teams are going to run against us but protections we get on pass [plays]."

And when you know what's coming it's easier to get to the quarterback. The Titans ranked seventh in the NFL with 40 sacks in 2007. "His presence in the run game is obvious," Fisher said. "But the pass rush involves two components: inside push and outside speed. You collapse the pocket but without the inside push, the quarterback can step up and miss the outside speed and make a play. The pocket collapses very quickly because of his presence, and he draws double teams, constantly drawing double teams. That creates one-on-ones for teammates and if they can win their share, you have in essence what we had last year, a great pass rush."

Haynesworth hasn't been without his share of petulant behavior. The low point came on Oct. 1, 2006, when he stomped on the head of helmetless Dallas Cowboys offensive lineman Andre Gurode at the end of a play. His cleat opened a gash on Gurode's face that required 30 stitches. The next day the NFL hit Haynesworth with a five-game suspension, the longest in NFL history for an on-field incident. He forfeited around $190,000 in salary as a result of five missed game checks, and he did not appeal the suspension, believing he deserved the full brunt of the punishment.

"What I did out there was disgusting," Haynesworth said at the time. "It doesn't matter what the league does to me. The way I feel right now, you just can't describe it."

Haynesworth apologized to Gurode and held a news conference to apologize to Titans fans and anyone who had watched the game. Gurode decided not to press criminal charges, and Haynesworth underwent anger-management counseling. With that hanging over his head, Haynesworth went out in 2007 and enjoyed his finest season. His hope was that it in some way atoned for his previous behavior.

"I didn't want last year's suspension to define my career," Haynesworth said. "The season I wanted to have this year was one to rewrite the history books on me so that people would remember me as a good football player, not for what happened last year, having the longest suspension. It was a difficult time in my life, but I was determined to keep working hard to get to this point and earn the respect of my teammates, coaches, and fans."

Haynesworth will play under the franchise-tag designation in 2008. That means the Titans can keep him under contract this year but must pay him an amount equal to or greater than the average of the top five salaries at his position or 120 percent of his previous year's salary, whichever is greater. Exclusive franchise players cannot negotiate with other teams.

"He was probably the most dominant defensive player in the league (in 2007)," Fisher said. "It has taken him some time to reach this level. He always had to deal with injuries. Right now he's in the prime of his career.

"We hope to keep him. Our expectations are that he will be able to retire as a Titan."

6

JEFF FISHER

by Bob McClellan

Jeff Fisher entered his 15th season as head coach of the Tennessee Titans in 2008.

By comparison, the Oakland Raiders have had eight head coaches since Fisher took the helm of the then-Houston Oilers from Jack Pardee with six games to play in the 1994 season.

With his combed-back black hair, thick mustache and youthful appearance, Fisher is the unquestioned face of the franchise. He may have reached the ripe old age of 50, but he still looks like he could play for a snap or two if needed. He has a passion for his job, a competitive fire that burns and flashes across his eyes every time he talks about the game and the men who play it.

But passion and coaching acumen alone don't explain a 15-year run with one franchise. Fisher boils it down to one key ingredient. "It's important that I can trust them and they can trust me," Fisher said. "I won't ask them to do something they can't do, but my

During the Titans' 10 years in Tennessee, there has been one constant: head coach Jeff Fisher. (Photo courtesy Tennessee Titans)

responsibility is to try to push them beyond their own expectations or their own limits, and do it in a subtle way.

"At the end of the day [the] most important thing is I want them to have fun. This is a game. You should pull into the parking lot and get out of your car and hustle in because you look forward to coming to work, even after tough losses on Monday, because you're gonna put it behind you and have a chance to win your next game. To my knowledge I don't know of anyone who has not looked forward to coming to work here, nor do I know a player who has left who didn't have an interest in coming back. That's not just about me, that's about the organization."

> **This is a game. You should pull into the parking lot and get out of your car and hustle in because you look forward to coming to work.**

Fisher began his coaching career more or less even before his playing career ended. A seventh-round pick out of the University of Southern California by the Chicago Bears in 1981, Fisher appeared in 49 games as a defensive back and return specialist in five seasons. None of those appearances took place in 1985, when the Bears made an incredible run to the Super Bowl behind coordinator Buddy Ryan's "46" defense. Fisher spent the 1985 season on injured reserve after an ankle injury prematurely ended his playing career. But he became an "unofficial" assistant to Ryan, and he earned a Super Bowl ring after the Bears completed an 18–1 season with a 46–10 thrashing of the New England Patriots in Super Bowl XX.

From there Fisher followed Ryan to the Philadelphia Eagles. The crusty, cantankerous Ryan landed the head-coaching job with the Eagles following the Super Bowl, and he brought his protégé with him to coach the defensive backs. Three years later, in 1988, Fisher was promoted, becoming the youngest defensive coordinator in the league. By 1989 he had fashioned quite a unit, one that led the NFL in interceptions and sacks. One year later, under Fisher's tutelage, the Eagles' defense led the NFL in interceptions (30) and quarterback sacks (62). The unit backed it up in 1990, ranking as the league's top rushing defense and coming in second in sacks.

Fisher left Philadelphia to serve as defensive coordinator for the Los Angeles Rams under John Robinson, Fisher's coach at USC. He spent the next two years as the defensive backs coach for the San Francisco 49ers before joining the Oilers' staff in 1994. They were looking for someone to replace Ryan, who had been the team's defensive coordinator in 1993 and had installed the 46 with great success. The Oilers had ripped off an 11-game winning streak that season, and it helped Ryan land another head-coaching job, with the Arizona Cardinals.

Fisher was steeped in the 46, so he came aboard under head coach Pardee. When Pardee resigned under pressure after a 1–9 start in 1994, Fisher was elevated to the top position. He immediately began putting his stamp on the program with the 1995 draft, when the Titans selected with their first pick, No. 3 overall, a quarterback out of Division I-AA Alcorn State by the name of Steve "Air" McNair. A year later, the Titans took the Heisman Trophy winner out of Ohio State with the 14th overall pick, a giant of a running back named Eddie George.

Jeff Fisher's steady hand helped guide Steve McNair to stardom. Now, he's doing the same with Vince Young. (Photo courtesy Tennessee Titans)

The three of them would be together for the next eight seasons. They would compile a remarkable 80–48 record and make four postseason appearances. They won the AFC Championship in 1999, and they played for it in 2002.

These were heady times in Nashville. Fisher had kept the team together through the difficult transition from a lame-duck year in Houston to moving the team to Tennessee, first to Memphis then to Vanderbilt Stadium in Nashville before the team took its permanent home at LP Field in 1999. After three consecutive 8–8 seasons, the Titans were ready to break out when they finally had a place to hang their hats. They also had a young quarterback and a young running back who already were asserting themselves, within the team and around the league.

"As we were building the team, Eddie was perfect because we were developing a young quarterback and when you develop a young quarterback, you need to run the football and rely on someone to run the football and steel the mentality," Fisher said. "We emphasized the run game and the toughness, and it allowed us to create an identity."

Fisher's philosophy always has been to run the football well and to stop the run. It's easy to understand why he has been so good and lasted so long when you consider how well his teams have done by those benchmarks. In 10 of the last 12 seasons, the Titans have finished in the top half of the NFL in rushing, including six top-10 finishes. They've been even stronger against the run, ranking in the top 10 in rushing defense in 10 of the last 13 seasons.

When you run the ball and stop the run, you're known as a tough team in the league. It's a mental edge that Fisher loves to have on his side. The players who have played for him call him a player's coach. Young enough to relate, accomplished enough to follow into battle.

"He's so unique in the fact he has that innate ability to adjust and change," tight end Frank Wycheck said. "He has certain philosophies that he goes by and certain ways he goes about things, but everything isn't etched in stone. He's willing to make adjustments to make things better. His message always stays fresh. That's why you can last. He's a guy whose message never gets old.

"There's a respect there. He can be cool with you, but you're never gonna cross the line and not respect what he's about."

For sure, there have been some tough stretches. The salary-cap era virtually dictates that there are going to be seasons that come along where your ability to win is going to be hampered by the financial structure of your team. It hit the Titans hardest in 2004 and 2005, when they lost several key players because they couldn't afford to keep them. Tennessee went 5–11 in 2004 and 4–12 in 2005. There even were rumblings about Fisher's job security. Team owner Bud Adams never wavered in his support for Fisher, however. He realized early that a winner was built on consistency, on not diverging from the path set forth.

"It starts with ownership. Mr. Adams understands the league, the game, he understands things change from year to year and he has been patient," Fisher said. "He understands we're here doing everything we can to win him a championship. That's hard to do and that's what motivates me.

"Every year I start out fresh and ready to go. I enjoy work and look forward to coming to work and I'm fortunate he's given me this opportunity. You're only as good the people around you, and I'm not just talking about the coaching staff, which is very good, but also the guards at the front desk to the grounds guys to the people in the stadium. Everyone is committed to winning. It's not just staff, it's everybody. When you're surrounded with good

Jeff Fisher's coaching philosophy has always centered on running the ball well and stopping the run.
(Photo courtesy Tennessee Titans)

people who don't have egos and are committed to doing the same thing, it makes the job easier. It's not an easy job, but it makes it easier."

Fisher has managed to be a disciplinarian without being heavy-handed and to be approachable without being a pushover. "My door is open. I want the players to feel they can come in anytime, not just when they're called in here," Fisher said. "When there is trust between me and the player then there is trust between the player and his teammate. That's ultimately what you need, that trust factor. When the guard can trust the tackle, then you have something good going. And when you have trust in the locker room, you have a solid locker room and you've got what ends up being good chemistry, and chemistry wins you ballgames."

Defensive end Jevon Kearse began his career under Fisher. A first-round pick by the Titans in the 1999 draft, he played his first five—and by far his most successful—seasons in Tennessee before signing with the Philadelphia Eagles as a free agent. After four seasons in Philly, he signed as a free agent…to make his return to LP Field. He says he can't wait to play for Fisher again.

"He's just able to adjust. He gets the right group of guys and the right coaches," Kearse said. "He makes the chemistry work.

"He's a player's coach. That's basically it right there. That's what brought me back. He said, 'We're bringing you back here to put you in a position to make plays, get back on the field, and prove to the world that you still have it.' I'm ready to go."

The Titans have been on an upswing the last two years after the dip in 2004-05. They went 8–8 in 2006 in what surely was one of Fisher's finest hours. The team started 0–5, meaning by that point it had won only nine of its last 37 games. Whatever heat was on the coach at the end of 2005 was nearing a boil. Somehow, Fisher guided the Titans back from the brink behind a rookie quarterback who had been the No. 3 pick overall, a young man named Vince Young. They won eight of their final 11 games, including a six-game winning streak, and missed the playoffs by one game. Young earned Rookie of the Year honors, and the offense posted the sixth-highest rushing total in franchise history, the second highest in the Fisher era (1997).

> **He's a player's coach. That's what brought me back.**

It was a very young team, the NFL's second-youngest, as a matter of fact. But it learned to win close games, going 7–4 in games decided by seven points or fewer (second-most wins in that category in the NFL) and six come-from-behind victories.

"That was amazing," said Wycheck, who retired after the 2003 season. "Any team would have packed it in. Jeff got the message through and they fought back."

It put Fisher and the franchise in a comfortable and familiar position: Young team, young quarterback, team on the rise. But times have changed, the coach says. It is, he believes, more difficult to reach young players these days.

"I think it takes a little more time to build the trust nowadays. The players are different," Fisher said. "There's a respect factor, not for the coach or position coach, but general respect factor for the game that over time may have begun to deteriorate. But I see it coming back. I see it coming back as a result of the commissioner's new personal conduct policy and those types of things.

"That NFL shield owes us absolutely nothing. All it does is provide us an opportunity. There is no better opportunity in pro sports than to be a part of this. When players understand that and the opportunity, they will define their own careers based on how they handle themselves. In those instances when maybe some of them aren't seeing as clearly as they should, they need to be reminded in a subtle way. Our job as coaches is to minimize mistakes. If I have a guy that is struggling and making mistakes and I put him on the field, it's not his fault, it's mine because I put him out there."

The NFL, for the first time, sent every player who was drafted in 2008 to visit the Pro Football Hall of Fame. Fisher loves the idea. "I think when they go I know they will be

One of the biggest reasons for Jeff Fisher's longevity as Titans coach is his ability to adapt to the changing attitudes of NFL players. (Photo courtesy Tennessee Titans)

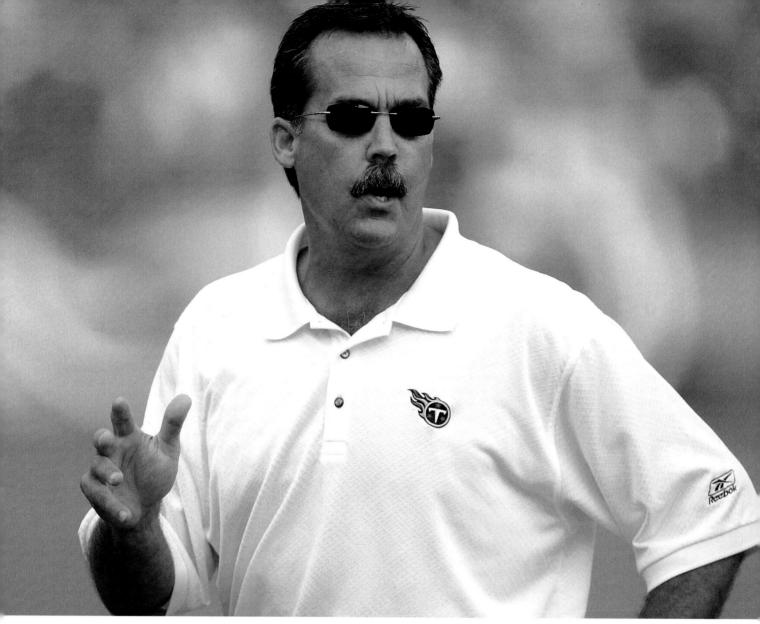

Jeff Fisher's longevity as Titans coach has helped the franchise build a tradition matched by few other teams in the NFL. (Photo courtesy of Tennessee Titans)

overwhelmed at the tradition of the game and the great players that have played before them who have paved the way," Fisher said. "They'll have more respect for and realize it's not only an honor to go to Canton, but to have a chance one day to have your bust in Canton.

"I just think because of where we are now, I think the younger players haven't been exposed to the older players and tradition and history and the great plays and the runs that some of these teams had, whether it was the Steelers, the 49ers, the Cowboys, the Buffalo Bills. To think the Bills went back to the Super Bowl four consecutive times knowing how hard it is to get there once. I think they'll come away with respect and appreciation for the game."

Years from now, those rookies may find another bust in Canton, one belonging to a graying coach with a thinning mustache. But if the sculptor captures the competitive fire that burns and flashes across his eyes, there will be no doubt as to the model for it.